**Nashua
Public
Library**

Enjoy this book!

Please remember to return it on time
so that others may enjoy it too.

Manage your library account and
discover all we offer by visiting us
online at www.nashualibrary.org

Love your library? Tell a friend!

WE FIND OURSELVES PUT TO THE TEST

We Find Ourselves
Put to the Test

A Reading of the Book of Job

JAMES CROOKS

McGill-Queen's University Press
Montreal & Kingston • London • Chicago

ISBN 978-0-7735-5315-6 (cloth)
ISBN 978-0-7735-5437-5 (ePDF)
ISBN 978-0-7735-5438-2 (ePUB)

Legal deposit second quarter 2018
Bibliothèque nationale du Québec

Printed in Canada on acid-free paper that is 100% ancient forest free
(100% post-consumer recycled), processed chlorine free

This book has been published with the help of a grant from Bishop's
University.

Funded by the   Financé par le
Government   gouvernement
of Canada   du Canada Canada Council   Conseil des arts
       for the Arts   du Canada

We acknowledge the support of the Canada Council for the Arts, which
last year invested $153 million to bring the arts to Canadians throughout
the country.

Nous remercions le Conseil des arts du Canada de son soutien. L'an dernier,
le Conseil a investi 153 millions de dollars pour mettre de l'art dans la vie
des Canadiennes et des Canadiens de tout le pays.

Library and Archives Canada Cataloguing in Publication

Crooks, James, 1959–, author
We find ourselves put to the test: a reading of the Book of Job/
James Crooks.

Includes bibliographical references and index.
Issued in print and electronic formats.
ISBN 978-0-7735-5315-6 (cloth). – ISBN 978-0-7735-5437-5 (ePDF). –
ISBN 978-0-7735-5438-2 (ePUB)

1. Job (Biblical figure). 2. Bible. Job – Criticism, interpretation, etc.
I. Title.

BS1415.52.C76 2018   223'.106   C2018-900249-2
                                             C2018-900250-6

This book was typeset by Marquis Interscript in 11/14 Sabon.

For Marge and Bob:
there are none like them on the earth ...

Contents

Preface: "Take Up and Read!"

"Thus much I uttered, weeping, in the most bitter contrition of my heart: whenas behold I heard a voice from some neighbour's house, as it had been of a boy or girl, I know not whether, in a singing tune saying, and often repeating: Take up and read, Take up and read."[1]

For almost twenty-five years now I've met with a handful of colleagues, students, and other fellow-travellers – on Friday afternoons, in the living room of a good friend – to read and discuss texts of mutual interest. In the 1990s, subject to the passion of the group's core members, we looked almost exclusively at Plato's dialogues. More recently, we've picked up a number of other works of classic philosophy and literature. Our meetings have taken a variety of forms. Sometimes discussions have been framed or led by an expert. Sometimes members of the group have presented embryonic versions of their own work. In the last seven or eight years, we have for the most part simply read aloud some passage (usually four or five pages) of whatever we're studying, and then weighed its contents. It's no exaggeration to say that for me these conversations – undertaken always in trust and friendship, founded on the conviction that the monuments of our intellectual tradition have in them something of inestimable value, that grappling with them will make us better teachers and better people – have been the most formative talks of my working life.

As I came within hailing distance of the end of a first draft of my reflections on the Book of Job, I asked my colleagues if they had any interest in hearing my work. Their response was typically generous – and so we agreed, for the first time in our long association, to read the Bible together. Not more than twenty minutes into our inaugural session, the challenges of this project had begun to emerge. The mists of history have created accidentally for the Book of Job the effect Plato sometimes orchestrates deliberately in dialogues such as the *Symposium* and the *Parmenides* – namely, a severing of the reported conversation from anything like verifiable historical events that could act as an independent standard for evaluating the statements and motivations of its participants. Although the consensus of scholars is that the Book of Job as we have it appeared between the seventh and fourth centuries BCE, there is, in the tradition of biblical exegesis, a lively debate as to its date of composition.[2] We do not know the identity of its author, or the pre-existent forms of the story he or she[3] may have been exposed to, adapted, or appropriated. Indeed, we can't be certain that we are dealing with a single writer, that what we have hasn't been amended substantially by generations of editors and copyists.

Then there is the poem itself. In the Hebrew Bible, it is part of the *Hagiographa* (Writings) sitting between Proverbs and The Song of Songs. In the Christian Bible, it is the first book of the so-called wisdom literature that also includes Psalms, Proverbs, and Ecclesiastes. Its forty-two chapters (a mere thirty-seven pages in the Revised Standard Version [RSV] I will be citing) comprise five episodes of unequal length: a prologue, with scenes alternating between heaven and earth, introducing God, Satan, and Job, and culminating in the destruction of our protagonist's property, the death of his children, and the loss of his health (Chapters 1–2); an extended dialogue between Job and three of his friends – Eliphaz, Bildad, and Zophar – who, having learned of his suffering, arrive to comfort him (Chapters 3–31); the speeches of a younger man – Elihu – who, overhearing that dialogue, thinks neither Job nor his friends have accounted properly the meaning of suffering (Chapters 32–37); an epiphany that arrives as a "voice from the whirlwind," in which God himself speaks (Chapters 38–41); and an epilogue, in which Job acknowledges the wonders God reveals to him and has his fortunes restored (Chapter 42). There is no page free of linguistic controversy. The

Hebrew text is in many places uncertain.[4] As a result, translators must speculate and often disagree. The philosophical/theological stakes here can be alarmingly high. To take but one example, the King James Version of the Bible renders 19:26 as:

> And though after my skin worms destroy this body, yet *in my flesh* shall I see God (italics mine).

The RSV reads:

> And after my skin has been thus destroyed, then *without my flesh* I shall see God (italics mine).

We made a point, in our discussions, of consulting and reading from a variety of translations. In addition, I always brought Robert Gordis's *The Book of Job: Commentary, New Translation, and Special Studies*.[5] Its verse-by-verse analysis gives you access to the wider frame of Biblical Hebrew and related ancient Near Eastern languages, marshalling very powerfully the resources of the scholarly tradition for cracking some of the text's most persistent linguistic riddles.

Still – and here I come to my real concern – the controversies regarding dates, authorship, and translation pale in comparison to the challenges presented by the Book of Job's substantive existential/philosophical contradictions: its portrait of a suffering that both destroys and ennobles the sufferer, of a God who both loves and abandons His faithful servant, of friends whose comfort culminates in rage, of a protagonist whose bitterness ferments, against all expectation, into patience. As our little group struggled with these contradictions, it became evident that our goal ought not to be the dream of eliminating them (in the sense of dissolving them into a scholarly account of the social and political forces at work in the poem's production, or of integrating them into a theological apologetic of suffering) but of finding a way to *own* them, of trying to articulate the truth that moves in them, of bringing them to life.

In the event, we took up pursuit of this goal in two ways: First, by simply reading the text aloud. It is surprising how powerful that is, following one translation while hearing another, listening to a specific human voice draw attention in performance to certain words and phrases, to particular features of a character, grasping both the propositions and the tone of an argument as it unfolds in real time. Each live reading provoked a kind of freeform discussion among us on everything from minute questions about vocabulary and the history of words to the most intractable theological problems. When we came to the end of the verses taken up in one of my chapters, I read that chapter. In this way, my own work, which was the trigger of our meetings, found its rightful place – behind performance of the poem and spontaneous dialogue with it; a moment of reflection and transition, of recreation, before returning to the matter itself. Second, we tried to own the Book of Job's substantial contradictions by "taking it up" as speaking directly to *our* sojourn through the failures, losses, endurances, and epiphanies of our own experience. In such a reading, you bring the text to life not by breathing your energies and imaginations into *it*, but by letting it animate *you* – by pondering, with the poet's help, your own narratives and communities, your own intellectual adventures, the limits of your own understanding, perhaps ultimately the possibility of your own encounter of the holy. The upshot of all of it for me is this: in a best possible world, a reading of the Book of Job would discover *you*, as the voices of children are said to have discovered Augustine in the garden at Milan, ready to marshal all the forces at your disposal for making sense of your life, the store of your learning and experience. And ready – if brought to the limit of what those forces compass at present – to revisit the ground of your own story.

Acknowledgments

This little book owes its safe arrival in the world to a number of midwives. I am grateful to the Senate Research Committee of Bishop's University for its material support. Mark Abley of McGill-Queen's University Press was extremely generous with his time, talent, and concrete feedback in guiding the manuscript through the editing process that began with its original review and culminated with its acceptance for publication. I am indebted, as well, to two anonymous readers for their thoughtful criticisms – many of which have been incorporated and have improved my work.

The book's title I take from an offhand remark of Cyril Welch's. He was my first teacher in philosophy and the person from whom I have learned the most, by far, in four decades now of devotion to that discipline. Benoit Bacon, Lynn Charpentier, Jenn Cianca, Bruce Gilbert, Leigh Jurecka, Christina Reimer, Dale Stout, and Harvey White read some or all of my original draft. I am deeply grateful for their friendship, support, and insight. Benoit, Jenn, and Dale were, in addition, my running partners as I worked out various parts of the argument I've tried to make. More than a few of their kilometres over the past couple of years have been kindly dedicated to discussion of its elements.

Beyond the orbit of strictly philosophical discussion, I have benefited greatly from the wisdom of colleagues and friends Michael Childs, Michael Goldbloom, Claire Grogan, Kerry Hull, Stuart McKelvie, Daniel Miller, Michele Murray, and Royal Orr.

Their own work, whether in teaching, research, or university governance, has been instructive and inspiring.

In facing what I take to be the Book of Job's central riddle, I draw heavily on experiences in the theatre – especially those as a sometime actor and musician in Spring Session Studio Theatre productions at Bishop's University. I thank George Rideout and Fannie Gaudette for their crucial roles in creating the world of those productions and Stephanie Izsak for lighting it up – first in shared projects, subsequently in conversations about acting and life.

Finally, and most importantly, I thank Willa Montague – my voice from the whirlwind on countless occasions over the past thirty-eight years and a daily reminder that love's accommodations outlast and encompass all of fortune's comings and goings.

WE FIND OURSELVES PUT TO THE TEST

Two Beginnings – or, How I Came to the Book of Job

A PHILOSOPHER'S QUESTIONS

The Book of Job is, among other things, an exercise in philosophy. It makes arguments. It deploys all the discursive resources of poetry, metre, metaphor, and popular rhetoric to establish and counter positions. It develops a play of characters as subtle and complicated as any we see in the Platonic *Dialogues*. It addresses a series of fundamental issues, including (but not limited to) moral integrity, suffering, human knowledge, justice, providence, divine love, and healing. Above all, it pursues the business of reflection at that depth reached perhaps only in the great beginning of our written culture, inviting our wonder in ways that carry us back to the intimate realm of what we might call our personal search for wisdom and understanding – a realm in which we feel ourselves addressed by the world, in which we find intermingled both the accreted layers of our reading and formal education and the accidents, exigencies, and epiphanies of our experience and our real human relations. The odd feeling of gratitude that comes with the struggle to make sense of the Book of Job (and what a struggle it is!) stems, I think, from the fact that it restores us to this intimacy, the real origin and sustaining draw of intellectual life.

Each such life has its fundamental questions, the enduring issues that shape it and prod it forward. You can often see them without much trouble in works of poets and writers whose explicit business consists in developing them directly and giving them a voice. With a little more spadework, you can uncover them as catalysts in the scholarly or scientific research that professors undertake in the practice of their disciplines. For philosophy, which stands always now somewhat uncomfortably between creativity and research, it seems to me that they produce what we might call an orientation or taste, not always – indeed, mostly not – by design or self-consciously. I remember being well into doctoral work on Martin Heidegger's *Nietzsche* volumes (drafting the final chapter in fact) before it became clear to me why I thought the wider world couldn't live without news of them. Later, gainfully employed and having fallen, as a result of one of those accidents of duty we come to appreciate in middle age, into teaching Plato to undergraduates, I had the same experience: profound sympathy, followed only considerably later by a clear sense of the source.

It was in both cases for me a single question, the chief concern, or perhaps better, the motivating anxiety of my own very modest intimate realm: Are we entitled to think of the world in which we find ourselves as a home or not? By this I mean something more than: Can we construct states or communities? Can we conceive and impose distinctively human values on a nature that is in important ways alien to us? It seems clear that we can do these things and that our having done them is the condition for the possibility of social science, cultural studies, art and its criticism, etc. What I want to know is in some sense more basic: Are we entitled to think of the world *itself* as welcoming, nurturing, sheltering, and loving?

Heidegger's answer to this question is already nested in the arguments of his masterwork, *Being and Time*, which privilege familiar places and things (workshops and tools, for example) and ask us to understand the ideas of science (such as the mathematical descriptions of space and time, or the conception of matter in contemporary physics) as derivative of, and ultimately dependent upon, experience of those places and things.[1] But he drives the point home explicitly and thematically only later on in his critique of modern metaphysics and its apotheosis in the age of technology.² In that age, he argues – *our* age – generations of presuming that spaces and times are essentially indifferent to us culminate in the reduction of all nature (including human nature) to the status of something like raw material. Confronting the reality of that reduction, cast out into it, we suddenly find ourselves homeless, without inherent dignity or any intrinsic right to dignified treatment, in a way that affronts both the intellectual spirit and the social and political institutions that make our age possible. The story of modernity is accordingly tragic. Its perfection or fulfillment is also its downfall. And it is bearable only because its own undoing reminds us that, as human beings, we are called to make ourselves at home.

One of the triggers of the technological age on Heidegger's account is the flight of the gods. Things and others show themselves to us in the devastated form of mere raw material only after all connections to heavenly powers have been severed, after our divinities have either packed up and left or been exposed as frauds. But we need not live in a godless era to find ourselves in a culture where the consensus is that the *cosmos* is indifferent to us or, indeed, that philosophy's first order of business is to resuscitate the argument that the world is at bottom accommodating. Looking back on the Homeric tradition, Plato felt called upon to counter a kind of malaise in the politics and intellectual life of fourth-century Athens, the source of which he construed at least in part as theological. Greek poetry was for him, among other things, an anthology of stories of divine neglect and abandonment. The upshot of those stories was that the gods simply didn't care whether human beings – mortals – found their temporary quarters hospitable or not, that they intervened with, favoured, punished, preserved, or destroyed their human sons and daughters indiscriminately.

In the *Republic*³ and elsewhere,⁴ Plato argues strenuously against this view. The absolute harmony of rationality and divinity is the condition for the possibility of soundly constituted souls. The constitution of the soul, in turn, may be mirrored in a city – the founding and preserving of which lets human beings perfect or realize precisely those possibilities of accommodation given to them by nature. The incontrovertible existential exclamation point on this argument is Socrates' hymn to the laws of Athens at the end of the *Crito*. In the very face of death, and despite its failure in his case to act in its best interest, he acknowledges as fundamental, as outstripping all other issues, the nurturing accommodation of the city of his birth.[5]

For a long time, I simply promoted these arguments – with my students, in conversations with friends and colleagues, and in published work. Heidegger seemed to me a powerful alternative both to post-Cartesian philosophies of knowledge and to the limited scientism of the Anglo-American philosophy that dominated the curricula of most North American universities for the better part of the twentieth century, sidelining or shooing away as nonsense many of the traditional questions of metaphysics, ethics, and aesthetics. The arguments of *Being and Time* and the lectures and essays of the 1930s, 1940s, and 1950s were a gust of fresh air, a reminder of how philosophy might be directly relevant to the comprehension of your own experience. Likewise, Plato seemed to me an antidote to the interminable criticism of constructivist and deconstructionist forms of postmodernism. In the Socrates of the *Dialogues*, we saw a character as subtle, as ironic, and as playful as a Derrida in his skewering of conventional wisdom, but devoted above all to finding his way back to the truth. His criticism always served a higher purpose.

But when, more than fifteen years ago now, at the prodding of others, in teaching adventures outside the Department of Philosophy and in further reading prompted at least indirectly by those adventures, I measured the sophistication of my Heideggerian/Platonic philosophical taste against the wider resources of the Western literary tradition, I found myself in a crisis of confidence. For in that wider tradition – a large tent that includes poetry, drama, Biblical prophecy, the work of the novel, investigative journalism, travel writing, diaries, biographies, autobiographies, opera, even musical settings of sacred texts – we find accounts of abandonment and devastation as fundamental to human life that reduce neither to shooing away alternatives nor to any kind of artificial ideological or academic criticism.

I remember, in particular, a kind of watershed event, the first of what were to become regular team-taught liberal arts foundation courses at my university focusing on broad themes in Western art and literature. Our subject that inaugural year was justice. A few weeks into the fall term, we undertook a study of Euripides' *Hecuba* under the guidance of a senior colleague from the Department of Classics.[6] The play recounts the fate of the wife (Hecuba) and children (Polyxena, Polydorus) of Priam, the patriarch whose kingdom is destroyed by Achilles, Odysseus, and the Greeks at the end of the Trojan War. In a careful reading of its dramatic sequences, my colleague showed us how deftly the playwright superimposes – like a translucent screen or a projection – the noble sacrifice of Polyxena on the bloody murder of Polydorus, evoking in the doubled image the idea that human civilization, for all its ceremonies and conventions, for all its attempts to accommodate strife and death in the elaboration and maintenance of a just and rational order, is but the mask of a barbarism worse (because of its hypocrisy) than that of the merciless animal kingdom.

Months later, near the end of the winter term, I myself contributed some lectures on Franz Kafka's *The Trial*. In the penultimate chapter of that uncannily accurate map of the twentieth-century mind, the protagonist, Joseph K., is accosted by a priest after ducking into the local cathedral to act as a tour guide for a visiting business associate. I was struck by the thought that the episode at once recalls and reverses the Gospel of John 20:11–18, where a resurrected Jesus reveals himself to Mary Magdalene. I say "recalls," because in both cases epiphany follows directly the surprise of being addressed unexpectedly by name. ("Jesus said to her, 'Mary.' She turned and said to him in Hebrew 'Rabboni!' [which means teacher]"; "it was no congregation the priest was addressing, the words were unambiguous and inescapable, he was calling out: 'Joseph K.!'")[7] I say "reverses," because the priest turns out to be the most eloquent agent of what Kafka calls "the Court" – the absolutely inscrutable body that has indicted K. as the novel opens and sanctioned his summary execution as it closes. I remember thinking that, while John uses the power of personal address to make evident the restoration of the familiar (Christ's return to his friends and disciplines, his triumph over abandonment and death), Kafka uses it to renounce such things. In the *Trial*, the church is the mouthpiece of a transcendental indifference, like the sacrificial ceremonies of the *Hecuba*, a pretty likeness of something at least apparently monstrous.

I found these doubling effects (sacrifice/murder, personal address as vindication of the familiar/personal address as prelude to its renunciation) unnervingly compelling. And, as is so often the case with something newly "discovered," I began to see them everywhere: in the double plot and dark familial duplicities of *King Lear*, in *The Great Gatsby*'s sad and distressingly timeless transparencies of the American dream, in the superimposition of bourgeois adultery upon racially motivated rape in J.M. Coetzee's *Disgrace*, even in the sublime beauty of the final chorus of Bach's magisterial *Christmas Oratorio* (which, trumpeting the birth of Jesus, nevertheless takes as its theme the chorale tune that stands at the centre of the *St Matthew Passion*). How could the kind of dark truth elicited in such works ever be reconciled with an understanding of the *cosmos* as fundamentally welcoming, nurturing, sheltering, or loving? How could I acknowledge these portraits of abandonment, of divine and human indifference – for purposes of my own education and in the process of educating others – without surrendering the possibility of the world as a home? Wouldn't accepting the insights of Euripides and Kafka require me to find my original philosophical taste naive? By the same token, wouldn't sticking somehow with Heidegger and Plato lead me to the conclusion that those who see abandonment and indifference at the bottom of things are guilty of excessive cynicism?

As a journeyman thinker, these are the questions – the worries – I bring to study of the Book of Job. Its protagonist asks, famously: "But where shall wisdom be found? And where is the place of understanding?"[8]

Responding, our author seems to suggest: in the play – taking the most philosophically serious sense of that word – between love and indifference. Indeed, my intuition is that part of the

Book of Job's towering greatness lies in its encompassing and communicating both the positions that I (and so many others) have been trying to puzzle out, in binding them together without diluting or synthesizing either and certainly without reducing one to the other. To accomplish something of this nature – a convincing portrait of human being both welcomed and cast out, at home and abandoned – requires an art almost impossible to imagine in the contemporary world. But that is one reason the great books of antiquity warrant unlimited reading. In any case, if you imagine the art of the Book of Job as a massive puzzle, even an idiosyncratic and non-scholarly commentary such as the one I'm about to undertake – prompted, as it is in part, by the desire to sort out the viability of my own philosophical teaching and learning – might place one or two pieces properly.

AN OLD FRIEND'S RESPONSE

It is late afternoon on a weekday – a Thursday if memory serves – near the end of August 2010. I am sitting on the couch in the living room of a house I have had occasion to visit six or seven times over the course of the last thirty years. The furniture – modest, functional, and chosen originally with some care (at least one piece, I recall being told, was made by a local craftsman) – seems to me exactly the same as on the occasion of my first visit as a university student in the late 1970s or early 1980s. Even its arrangement is unchanged: couch against the back wall in front of a large window, table across to the left, to the right a chair from the same "set," angled kitty-corner, marking an invisible boundary between the living room and the hallway leading to home offices and bedroom. Sitting there across from me is the owner of the house, my first philosophy professor and one of perhaps four or five flesh-and-blood human beings I would claim as "teachers," reserving that word for people who actually open up the world to you and convince you to claim its wonders as your own. We have just returned from an extended lunch at a popular outdoor café on the main street of the town. Strolling between the two places I had remarked on changes to the neighbourhood and the campus: the new businesses, the looming closure and possible demolition of the United Church, the conversion of the old residence in which I had spent my first year of study to a modern centre for student services. A contrast, I now observe silently, to this familiar space, the physical appointments of which seem to be making a determined stand against the passage of time. The window behind me, the room's main source of natural light, looks out on a heavily wooded area that continues down the hill to an old quarry in which students occasionally used to swim. Today the still-brilliant summer sun is playing through the trees, making the kind of shifting patterns on the rug between us that you normally associate with reflections in water. Their movement toward the far wall in the first fifteen minutes or so of our conversation suggests that it will soon be time to turn on the lamp beside me.

I am sad. A year ago, over dinner on the porch of my cottage, he had told me that his wife of some forty-five years was terminally ill, no longer able to make the trip from their summer house in Luxembourg to their winter (school-term) house in New Brunswick. I had never known the two of them as anything but constant companions (indeed, that meal may have been the first time I had ever seen him socially without her) and I tried to tiptoe back and forth that evening, in the emotion-averse confines of my own mind, between acknowledging his news as fact and holding out hope of some rally or remission. At today's lunch he had made it clear that this was not in the cards. Her death was imminent. He was here briefly to set some affairs in order. Then … back to Luxembourg to face the end.

The gravity of such a circumstance pulls everything toward it. In its orbit, the quiet beauty of the hour becomes achingly fragile. The summer that stretched out before me in May and June, an invitation to reading, recreation, and modes of creativity the work year make almost impossible, suddenly addresses me like someone dear saying goodbye. The town's development appears to have taken hold at the price of eroding and effacing the place of my youth – the little world of undergraduate study, full of epiphanies and teachers at the height of their powers. And the house itself, doing its level best to resist these transformations, in the very constancy of its arrangement – her Canadian reading and her unfinished projects lie waiting for her on her desk in the room down the hall, as no doubt they have every year for decades – announces itself to me as the place where she is not and will not be again. I look at him, up to his neck now in the slowly fading dance of sun and shadows, recalling a line of Dante's that she had integrated into one of her own poems: "There is no greater sorrow than thinking back upon a happy time."[9]

I'm a poor comforter. I tried not to duck acknowledgment of his suffering – let alone hers – when he updated me at the café. But riding a fifty-year run of dumb luck, my own life has given me very little that is relevant to holding up my end of conversations about death and loss. And so I'm now trying to carry on as usual. Having settled myself on the couch, I've been yakking for the past twenty minutes about the eccentricities and failures of academic life, a subject I find pleasant, reassuringly light, and (ironically for me at present) conducive to affirmation of a point I'd heard him make on many occasions over the course of his working years: namely, that things would go better in universities if their faculties and administrations could pay more attention to what experience itself shows them. In the shorthand of our decades-long conversation, I sum up a tale I've been telling about the utility-driven follies of my university's current planning with the rhetorical question: "Where's the voice from the whirlwind?" By which I mean to ask: Why can't we set aside the dismal abstractions of middle management and focus on the beauty of what our traditions actually tell us about the world?

Funny: by means of this diversionary shoptalk we have come to the Book of Job. Picking up my reference, he tells me that he has begun to read the Hebrew Bible out loud. It helps him recover the real spirit of the text, he says. I respond that a colleague once told me that the Book of Amos may originally have been recited in public (like Homer's epics), then venture the opinion that the Book of Job itself might be effectively adapted for the stage, adding by way of illustration that a properly crafted scripting of the wager between God and Satan, together with its immediate consequences (Chapters 1 and 2), would be as spectacular an overture as any playwright could imagine. As he reflects on this, I "storyboard" the drama of the opening scene: the crisp shifts of venue between heaven and earth could be blocked on different levels of our set and separated further by lighting effects. Our "God" would somehow have to hold together what a contemporary audience could only interpret as the discord between loving pride in Job's exemplary service and apparent indifference to his virtual destruction – a tall order for any actor. Our "Satan," on the other hand, nothing if not consistent, would have the pleasure of channelling Shakespeare's Iago or Goethe's Mephistopheles, exploring the darker possibilities of logic and generally pouring poison in his master's ear. Finally, the challenge of our director would be to find a way to make the strange disconnects and ironies of the piece's beginning, the play of revelations (between God and Satan) and concealments (from Job and his doomed household), frame the remainder of the dialogue – the extended theological debate between Job and his friends that culminates in God's breaking the seal between heaven and earth.

"Yes," he says, responding specifically to the idea that the beginning of the Book of Job both reveals and conceals. "It's not that God announces either his wager or his permission to Satan to torment Job. All of that is invisible and utterly inaccessible. Job simply finds himself put to the test." Then, leaning forward slightly into the gloom that now separates us (in the course of our talk the light has faded to such an extent that it is no longer possible to make out clearly the expression on his face), shattering the pretense of mere academic conversation and marshalling quietly the sorrow of the hour and the season, the town and the house, he says: "That's how it is. We find ourselves put to the test."

More than a year later, ready to weigh the verses of the Book of Job and try to take its measure, I keep returning to this statement. He was right of course. Some misfortunes seem born of human foolishness and explainable in human terms. We tell ourselves that we can account quite well for the punishment of criminals and the comic misadventures of idiots. Even the fall of a hero seems to us governed by a set of psychological laws which, brought to life by an Aeschylus or a Sophocles, make it seem as inevitable and predictable as the behaviour of bodies in motion. But for the most part, what we think of as suffering simply arrives out of the blue: one day the child you hoped for and cherished is killed by a careless driver; one day the mother who taught you to love your world finally loses hers to Alzheimer's; one day the husband who by all accounts had everything to live for commits suicide; one day the retirement you planned with care and looked forward to is pulverized by the diagnosis of a terminal illness. In other times and places, the destructive force of such things has been almost imponderably terrifying: famines have wiped out populations indiscriminately; armies and militias have murdered whole towns and villages; in the very worst cases, states have set up factories of targeted mass death and genocide. Yet these inhuman horrors too, the scope of which makes thought and language tremble, aggregate the stories of individuals who one day found themselves thrown into a trial the severity and pain of which they could not deflect, overtaken by a test indifferent to their integrity as persons, to their very lives.

It's no exaggeration to say that nothing has been more vexatious to philosophy and theology in the West than the *fact* of this being thrown. That's because to offer explanations of it, as both philosophers and theologians are wont to do, actually effaces its essence – namely, our having been *overtaken*, our *finding ourselves* put to the test. The suffering that arrives out of the blue, thought of in terms of the way it presents itself to us in experience, has no antecedent causes. This, as we'll see, is a real bone of contention between Job and his friends, whose attempts at comfort reduce under the pressure of his objections to the presumption that his fall must have been precipitated by a cause of some kind (i.e., a moral failure). But even if, armed with the backstage pass to the machinations of the heavenly court that our author gives in the book's first two chapters, we describe Job's suffering as innocent or unprovoked, we set it back into an account of the order of things that does violence to the experience *he* has, which is first and foremost that of a pain seizing him without reason or purpose, threatening him perhaps above all because it is in principle incomprehensible. Part of the allure of my old friend's summary line is its evocation of this incomprehensibility as a non-negotiable reality: "That's how it is ... " As if those simple words exhausted completely the possibility of a further account.

But though the "test" that arrives out of the blue resists explanation, it remains possible to describe it. And indeed, to anticipate a central point of the commentary I want to make: We should read the Book of Job not as an explanation of suffering but as something closer to a phenomenological description – which is to say, an account of the way in which suffering makes itself manifest, shows itself, or comes to light.[10] The finer points of this account need to be developed in dialogue with the text. But I want to offer three provisional observations on the heels of what I've just said, with a view to getting my stories straight and making my own orientation in that dialogue as clear as possible:

First, suffering appears to destroy what you might call the refuge of personal history. In the course of your daily life, your "happy" life if I can put it that way, this history stands in a kind of seamless continuity with your present. Every morning, you return to the work you've been doing for x number of months or years. It may not always go well. But there is a kind of order and promise in it that reflects your input and helps you to find your place in things, to know yourself. Every night, you return to the bosom of your family or to those friends with whom you are, in one way or another, intimate. There may be stress there from time to time. But those to whom you are close are accorded their places of privilege in your heart because they continue to welcome you in the world. In both cases, the past is in a certain sense in front of us, alive with possibility and so real – lived and re-lived, inhabited. When you find yourself put to the test, you lose this accommodation. Think of the trauma of physical pain: in it, you are assailed by the absolute tyranny of the present. The comfort and ease of the past seems to dissolve completely, to *be* nothing. It's no accident that in constructing Job's ordeal Satan promotes bodily suffering as the ultimate test: "Skin for skin! All that a man has he will give for his life. But put forth thy hand now, and touch his bone and his flesh, and he will curse thee to thy face" (2:4–5).

The assault of an absolute and unforgiving present is also characteristic of grief. But it seems to me that this kind of pain makes transparent, in addition, the substance of the living past. It lies precisely in those possibilities *negated in your loss*. A past that is only past, no matter how beautiful, fulfilling, or loving, offers you no place to stand *now*.

Secondly, suffering appears to destroy what you might call the refuge of universality. In the course of your daily life, this universality is a kind of template for experience that confirms the basic intelligibility of the world and reconciles you to the necessities of your nature. With respect to the former, for example, you recognize that everything that happens to you has a cause and that every action you contemplate will have consequences. With respect to the latter, you understand that all human beings are mortal, that virtually all of us – even the most prudent and good-hearted people – experience reversals of fortune from time to time, that it would be a miracle to get through life without facing the deaths of at least some of the people closest to you, and so on. But when you find yourself put to the test, this knowledge seems spectral and worthless. In physical pain, you are assailed by the absolute tyranny of individuality. Your doctor's diagnosis of the origin of the cancer that now has you in its grip does nothing to alleviate your anguish. Nor does it help to ponder the fact that all bodies eventually break down. In grief, it doesn't help to hear that death is part of life, that it was his or her time to go, or indeed that everything happens for a reason. Universal truths of this kind are ghostly in comparison with the reality of the individual you loved. When I was a child, my mother would say to us sometimes, "You mean the world to me." As if the substance of the universal nested somehow in our little bodies. "As if," I say. But that's how it is …

Now ask yourself what you depend on in the course of your daily life – other than universality and personal history – to make yourself at home in the world. Universality is something like the template of human experience, personal history the content it organizes and forms. At a glance, there seems to be nothing that doesn't reduce to one of these categories. And if this is the case, then to lose them as anchors of sense and meaning is to lose your humanity. That many victims of suffering experience just such a loss is beyond question. That it is in many cases utterly overwhelming, physically and emotionally, history and literature demonstrate. (I keep thinking of Job's original children simply crushed under the house that falls on them, or his servants murdered by Satan's emissaries.)

But – and this would be my third observation – in cases of those who somehow *bear* suffering for a time, and certainly in the case of a person like Job himself who manages to survive it, something else is in play, a kind of endurance that sustains you even as the comforts of personal history and universality withdraw. I'd been struggling to find even a provisional expression of what's at stake in such endurance – it seemed to me more basic than either hope or confidence, for example, in the sense that it did not require belief in a better future – when I remembered a passage from Spinoza's *Ethics*. It comes near the beginning of the section dedicated to the philosophy of the emotions, effectively setting the stage for subsequent analyses of all determinate mental states: "The *conatus* with which each thing endeavors to persist in its own being is nothing but the actual essence of the thing itself."[11]

Spinoza's keyword *conatus* has a range of meanings – striving, exertion, or struggle, but also impulse, inclination, or tendency. He uses it here to capture and extend an idea already well established in Western philosophy, namely that, in the face of nature's hostility, living beings make every effort to keep on living.[12] I say Spinoza extends this idea because, unlike his Latin-speaking forbears, he grasps in *conatus* a universal metaphysical principle. On the argument of the *Ethics*, all modes of existence (whether organic or inorganic, extended or incorporeal) endeavour to persist in their own being. This persistence is not simply a property that things happen to *have*. Rather, *conatus* is Spinoza's name for what things *are*, for what he calls their "actual essence." But if that is the case, what we ought to anticipate in any complete or adequate phenomenology of suffering – beyond description of the withdrawal of the refuges of personal history and universality – is a portrait of the endurance that constitutes the nature of being itself. If Spinoza is right, the story of suffering can never rest simply or even finally on reports of destruction and abandonment. It must bring to light also the resiliency of *conatus*, the striving to make a stay in the world, to establish and defend a place, no matter what. It must deliver, in one way or another, the insight that what characterizes a thing or a person, above all, is an indomitable will to accommodation, a natural impulse to find and preserve shelter precisely in being the being that it/she/he is.

It seems to me that the idea of a naturally constitutive *conatus* captures, at least provisionally, the dignity of those who endure in suffering without hope or confidence. They do not will or wish for something impossible naively – in denial of the extremity of their situations. On the contrary, beyond all willing, wishing, accepting, and denying, they are stripped to the marvellous integrity of their being – a being that is itself the activity of a self-establishing, self-preserving struggle to settle into life and make themselves at home in it. In precisely this sense, the enduring sufferer is the model of humanity.

AN HYPOTHESIS FOR READING

"That's how it is," said my old friend, on the authority of his own sadness. "We find ourselves put to the test." In what follows, I want to suggest that the steadfast, unblinking, and utterly unsentimental description of just this experience constitutes the greatness of the Book of Job. In it, if my provisional account or something close to it can be justified by a more detailed reading of the text, you are simultaneously cast out (of the refuge of personal history, of the refuge of universality) *and* welcomed (by the *conatus* that embraces you, that *is* you, and so can never be taken from you as long as you live), abandoned *and* at home. My wager is that if we begin with this existential contradiction, looking to our author not for an explanation of it (for some kind of causal account) but rather a phenomenology – a careful description of the manner in which the contradiction presents itself – we'll see how love and indifference are at play in suffering, at stake in genuine wisdom and understanding, and at one in the "voice from the whirlwind."

Job Finds Himself Put to the Test

JOB'S FIRST WORDS

Its dramatic appeal notwithstanding, discussion of the wager between God and Satan described in Chapter 1 will have to wait. If I were simply to begin with it, I'd be hard pressed to present it to you as anything other than an explanation of the suffering that follows. Looking, instead, for something like a description of how suffering presents itself, I need to begin with Job, a person living a life like yours and mine, with no privileged access to the heavenly court. I need to ask how our author represents *his* experience, how he retraces the constitution of suffering not from the God's-eye view but from the perspective of the sufferer.

Part of the answer to this question is straightforward. It consists in the description of Job's misfortunes, leaving aside for the moment their attribution to the agency of Satan. The loss of children and possessions surfaces first, in a rapid-fire series of bulletins – 1:13–19 – the frame of which you needn't alter at all:

Now there was a day when his sons and daughters were eating and drinking wine in their eldest brother's house; and there came a messenger to Job, and said, "The oxen were plowing and the asses feeding beside them; and the Sabeans fell upon them and took them, and slew the servants with the edge of the sword; and I alone have escaped to tell you." While he was yet speaking, there came another, and said,

"The fire of God fell from the heaven and burned up the sheep and the servants, and consumed them; and I alone have escaped to tell you." While he was yet speaking there came another and said, "The Chaldeans formed three companies, and made a raid upon the camels and took them, and slew the servants with the edge of the sword; and I alone have escaped to tell you." While he was yet speaking, there came another, and said, "Your sons and daughters were eating and drinking wine in their eldest brother's house; and behold, a great wind came across the wilderness, and struck the four corners of the house, and it fell upon the young people, and they are dead; and I alone have escaped to tell you."

The loss of Job's health is reported in the next chapter – 2:7–9. Although the author makes the role of Satan here explicit ("So Satan went forth ... and afflicted Job"), we can isolate the results of his work:

Job [was afflicted] with loathsome sores from the sole of his foot to the crown of his head. And he took a potsherd with which to scrape himself and sat among the ashes. Then his wife said to him, "Do you still hold fast to your integrity? Curse God and die."

Here is "the test": a series of misfortunes, each of which strikes closer to the core of Job's being. They are events with the kind of objective content reported in newspapers. And, their scope and temporal proximity aside, they arrive for him as they might for anyone with possessions, family, and personal health. Reading the accounts, you sympathize immediately. In your own life, you will have experienced similar losses or worried about incurring them. You know what the material constituents of human happiness are, and that they are fragile.

The representation of how Job "finds himself" in the face of his losses, however, is bound to strike you as far more subtle. That's because it already sets before you the author's central problem. Let me frame this problem – begin to develop it – provisionally, in reference to the first three statements he puts in the mouth of his protagonist:

After the last of the prototypes for Melville's Ismael delivers his dismal news, Job says: "Naked I came from my mother's womb, and naked shall I return; the Lord gave, and the Lord has taken away; blessed be the name of the Lord" (1:21).

Here is a motto for future Stoics. In apparent contradiction of the thumbnail sketch of suffering I offered above, our protagonist makes a show of taking refuge in universality. Individual loss is a moment of divine providence – part of the divinely designed cycle of birth and death, growth and decay. A pious person ought to praise that design, even if it unfolds at the cost of his own comfort.

In response to his wife's bitter counsel to "curse God and die," Job replies: "You speak as one of the foolish women would speak. Shall we receive good at the hand of God, and shall we not receive evil?" (2:10).

There is an important trace of affection or fellow-feeling in this otherwise harsh exchange.[1] Blaming someone for acting the fool, for talking *as if* they were a fool, makes sense only on the assumption that they are capable of better. The precise form of Job's admonishment holds open the possibility that his wife is only voicing the despair of his situation, that he and she might still stand together, in spite of her call for the curtain to come down. In apparent contradiction of my thumbnail sketch above, our protagonist holds on to the refuge of personal history. Unforgiving as she is, Job still regards his wife as someone capable of taking to heart the hard truth of God's providence. And his question, perfectly consistent with his first statement, urges her to do so.

But – and here is the problem – a mere five verses later, breaking the silence with his comforters, who have in the meantime made their arrival, Job cries: "Let the day perish wherein I was born, and the night which said, 'A man-child is conceived'" (3:3).

There follows – again in apparent contradiction of my remarks on *conatus* above – a rhetorical storm, the sole purpose of which is thoroughgoing self-renunciation. Its final words are particularly telling in relation to the philosophical tone of the first two interventions: "I am not at ease, nor am I quiet; I have no rest; but trouble comes" (3:26).

The experience of this shift is absolutely jarring. In about thirty seconds of reading time the author takes his character from the tranquil rationality to existential nausea – from a kind of proto-Stoicism to Jean-Paul Sartre and beyond.

At first glance, you're tempted to interpret this apparent dis-continuity as a failure of compositional vision. You might have been persuaded to forgive the author his portrait of God in the opening scene – simultaneously proud of and indifferent to his loyal servant. Theology, after all, is largely speculative. In a sym-pathetic frame of mind, you can imagine that this synthesis of attitudes appealed somehow to a mix of religious sensibilities in the original audience for the Book of Job. Job himself, though, is a human being. And all your experience tells you that human character is, at least ordinarily, more consistent. Not only that. The one thing you know about our protagonist on the basis of the opening scene is that he has a reputation for integrity (it drives his wife to distraction!) How in the world is such a reputation reconcilable with a sudden radical swing from proto-Stoicism to existential nihilism? It's an important question. If you can't appre-hend a unity in the representation of how Job "finds himself" in the face of his losses that runs deeper than, and accounts for, its apparent discontinuity, you'll be unable to trust the author to guide you through the phenomenology of suffering. And once that happens, you'll be tempted to undermine the dignity of your own work as a reader, insisting like a litigator on what Ralph Waldo Emerson once called "foolish consistency"[2] instead of expanding the frontiers of your own understanding.

THE GRAVITY OF SILENCE

What you have, then, on the evidence Job's first three statements is a hermeneutic puzzle – a kind of mystery that stands between you and a clear idea of the psychological disposition our author wants to represent. Among other things, this means that as a reader you're called upon almost immediately to play detective

– a popular occupation, as it turns out, in the scholarly world
of ancient texts. Here, and in a number of similar cases we'll see
later on, it seems to me crucial that you try to interpret our
author's work generously, that you trust him to surprise and con-
found you for good reasons, until such time as the accumulated
evidence makes it seem foolhardy to continue. In this spirit, consider at least provisionally two questions: Are there grounds for
interpreting the apparent shift in Job's attitude and emotional
state between 2:10 and 3:3 as part of a deliberate compositional
strategy? If so, to what advantage?

We know that, as with virtually all narratives of the Hebrew
Scriptures, the story of Job predates our author's version. It seems
to have circulated in various forms and languages throughout the
ancient Near East, one of numerous tales of "complaint and rec-
onciliation."3 The scholarly consensus is that what is original in
the Biblical account is the elaborate dialogue between Job and his
friends – that is, the theological argument that is settled in spectacular fashion by the arrival of God himself, the "voice from the
whirlwind." The ground of this consensus seems to me reasonable and at least partially evident even in English translations.
The style and tone of the dialogue – an extremely subtle portrait
of conversation, personality, and emotional fluctuation – stands
in marked contrast to what comes before and after – an account
of events which, though artfully constructed, retains the austerity
of expression, the simplicity, the stone-like impenetrability, characteristic of stories polished by the retelling of many generations.
In the original Hebrew the distinct character of these sections
is emphasized further by an obvious difference in metrics.4 The
introduction and the epilogue are written in prose, the dialogue
in verse. Now – the first and second of Job's statements (1:21,
2:10) belong to the prose introduction. But the third (3:3) is the
overture to the dialogue. If the author has taken the trouble to
separate these movements of his work stylistically, tonally, and
metrically, if indeed this is his contribution to the preservation of
his source material, then it seems possible, perhaps even likely,
that he will want to bring Job's speeches into the service of that

distinction, that his portrait of Job will be sketched in terms of the fundamental division of the text itself and in harmony with it.

It is of course more difficult to stipulate convincingly the goal of this strategy. It seems reasonable, though, to assume that our author is trying to open up the original tale and clarify its meaning, and that the contrast of styles, tones, and metrics – deliberate as it is – is meant to aid that clarification; that we apprehend the message of this version of the Job story precisely by attending to the ways in which the prose and dialogue sections rub against, illuminate, and/or bleed into each other. If these assumptions are valid, moreover, it's hard to avoid the conclusion that the transitions between the original tale and our author's addition – first at 2:11–13, then in Job's final utterances at 40:2–5 and 42:2–6 – play a special role. In terms of the hypothesis we're entertaining they would define the frontiers and transfer points of the play. Indeed, if you imagine the text – for purposes of pondering the full force of its compositional principle – as a kind of linguistic sculpture, they would be its points of contact with the ground, called upon to bear the weight of the entire structure, supporting or subtending all other verses and interventions. Among other things, that means: interpreting those verses and interventions would amount, ultimately, to making evident the ways in which they push down on the transitions. And indeed, the closer the material to be interpreted stands to the contact points, the more definitive for them that pressure would be. Needless to say, Job's opening statements stand in close proximity to 2:11–13. The second and third literally frame it. So, if we're right, the apparent discontinuity in the representation of how Job "finds himself" in the face of his losses (1:21, 2:10, 3:3) is an effect of the gravity of 2:11–13. And the solution to our hermeneutic puzzle depends on whether and to what extent we can find the resources to gauge that effect. Let's see if we can make some headway. Here is the text:

Now when Job's three friends heard of all this evil that had come upon him, they came each from his own place, Eliphaz the Temanite, Bildad the Shuhite, and Zophar the Naamathite.

They made an appointment together to come to condole with him and comfort him. And when they saw him from afar, they did not recognize him; and they raised their voices and wept; and they rent their robes and sprinkled dust upon their heads toward heaven. And they sat with him on the ground seven days and seven nights, and no one spoke a word to him, for they saw that his suffering was very great.

Note first that the themes of personal history, universality, and *conatus*, in the sense of persistence or endurance, return in this passage as inversions of the positions implied in Job's own statements – doubling effects of more or less the same kind you see in Euripides' *Hecuba* or Kafka's *The Trial*. In contrast to the calming rationalization he offers his wife at 2:10, the arrival of Eliphaz, Bildad, and Zophar confirms the extraordinary nature of his troubles. Their journeys – themselves fraught with risk and inconvenience – are justified only by the depth of his personal loss. Indeed, they offer him their friendship, at least initially, as shelter from a storm that has destroyed virtually everything else to which he might have turned for comfort and reassurance. In contrast to the proto-Stoic equanimity of Job's famous first words at 1:21 – "the Lord gave, and the Lord has taken away" – the ceremonies of mourning triggered by the sight of him while still at a distance suggest a scene so monstrous it blurs the distinction between life and death, a condition so pathetic it subverts the deepest categories available to us for making sense of the world. Finally, in contrast to the complete exasperation with suffering expressed at 3:3, the passages of time both implied and stipulated in 2:11–12 suggest an almost superhuman threshold of pain. It would have taken days, perhaps weeks, for word of Job's misfortunes to reach his friends; days, perhaps weeks, for them to agree on a coordinated intervention; days, perhaps weeks, to make the journey from their respective communities to the land of Uz. Through all this he has somehow persisted.

The play of these inversions or doublings against Job's initial statements is part of the puzzle already visible in the statements themselves. We need to keep working at a solution. As I said before, it seems key in producing an adequate description how Job "finds himself" qua sufferer. On the way back to that, though, I want to draw your attention to something else – something new and utterly compelling – in our weight-bearing transitional passage. It comes in the last sentence, attesting the old saying that the sting is in the tale: "And they sat with him on the ground seven days and seven nights, and no one spoke a word to him, for they saw that his suffering was great" (2:13).

In a work dominated by the theological dispute between Job and his comforters that spans 36 of its 42 chapters, you might easily pass over the stage direction given here. All the same, it is dramatically spectacular. Eliphaz, Bildad, and Zophar sit with Job for seven days and nights *in silence*. The duration of this vigil dwarfs that of the ensuing dialogue. If you allot the latter a reading time of two hours, it is roughly eighty-four times as long. Among other things, this means: in the dimension of real time, the Book of Job is first and foremost the representation of a wordless communion. What it gives you to think about, beyond (and before) the wager between God and Satan, beyond (and before) the arguments dedicated to decoding its consequences, even beyond (and before) the epiphany that brings the story to its climax, is a long silence. The text itself makes this point with the economy so characteristic of the Hebrew Scriptures: "no one spoke a word to him, *for they saw* that his suffering was great." As if it were understood that the spectacle of suffering *requires* us to stop talking; and that, accordingly, no description of it, phenomenological or otherwise, could ring true without recognizing and reflecting this requirement. "As if," I say. But that's how it is. The suffering of others leaves you at a loss for words, not only because, like me, you may have avoided for a time the blows of fortune, but because its theatre is wordless. The author of the Book of Job knows and says directly what life teaches us little by little: the spectacle of suffering calls for silence, unfolds in silence, shows itself in silence. Here is the key to our hermeneutic puzzle. To what, exactly, does it give us access?

Someone with a good deal of scholarly ambition and an encyclopedic knowledge of Western arts and letters should write for us someday *The Big Book of Silences* – the compendium of all cases, circumstances, and situations recorded in the poetry and prose of those traditions in which some character decides not to speak a word. The chapter on the Hebrew Bible would be a substantial piece in its own right. Consider, for example, the strange story Nadab and Abihu reported in Leviticus.[5] They are devoured by divine fire, apparently for making an unholy offering. Surveying this family tragedy, the writer tells us, their father Aaron simply "held his peace."[6] Or the Book of Amos, as dark in its own way as the Book of Job, where the prophet presents an enraged God for whom silence is nothing less than apocalyptic ("'Behold, the days are coming,' says the Lord God, 'when I will send a famine on the land; not a famine of bread, nor a thirst for water but of hearing the words of the Lord.'"[7]).

The chapter on philosophy would be shorter. But our scholar could certainly count on Plato's Socrates for some contributions. In the *Apology* he presents the silence of his *daimon* – the spiritual guide who provides important counsel to him on other occasions – as evidence of the fact that his defence is well-conceived and well-argued ("nor at any point in any part of my speech did the divine sign oppose me"[8]). At the end of the *Symposium*, in one of literature's most finely crafted comic scenes, the drunken Alcibiades, extemporizing a eulogy, challenges him to interrupt the moment he's played false. But Socrates holds his tongue, leaving us to ponder how the younger man's rambling summary of his intellectual seductiveness, a power he understands only inasmuch as he finds himself in its clutches, might be entirely true nevertheless.[9]

Add to this the almost infinite variations on what Kierkegaard calls aesthetic concealment[10] – lovers who hide things for each other's benefit, enemies who plot against each other in secret, orators whose power of discernment consists as much in choosing what to leave unsaid as in developing their themes positively – and you have an impressively diverse range of discursive phenomena: silences human and divine, possible and necessary, sincere and ironic, innocent and malevolent. The one thing they have in common is that they are *telling* silences. Indeed, their differences notwithstanding, these and other examples bring to your attention the fact that every silence has a determinate meaning, a communicative power.

In what does that power consist? Returning to the image I brushed by when introducing our weight-bearing transitional passage above: it consists of something like a discursive gravity. This gravity – as regards silence at least – displays three characteristics or moments: the draw of spoken words into the orbit of something unspoken, the charge of those words with a weight proportionate to that unspoken thing's reality, and the binding together of thoughts or ideas that, simply spoken, would fly apart in contradiction. We can sample each of these moments in the reticence of Job's comforters reported at 2:13.

Whatever they will have said to each other – in the correspondence occasioned by the discovery of their friend's misfortunes, on the way to visit him, in the lament triggered by the sight of his suffering at a distance – comes to rest in their wordless communion. Or again: their reticence is the manifest outcome of their discursive project, the actual expression of their solidarity.

As you'll see when we take a closer look at the arguments that make up the body of the text, that is not nothing. On the contrary, human comfort reaches the pinnacle of its dignity at 2:13. It is never subsequently as substantial, as profound. Eliphaz, Bildad, and Zophar are at their best, their most genuine, their most consoling, in silence, as if the unspoken itself were the measure of their success.

"As if," I say. But the fact is that their reticence gathers and represents for them and for us precisely the contradiction of suffering I sketched provisionally in the introduction. Silent, they bear witness both to the destruction of Job's worldly accommodation (the refuge of his personal history, the refuge of human universality) and to the persistence of his self-establishing, home-making, life-affirming *conatus*.

Let's defer for a moment the question of what conscious intentions might accompany this witness. We'll have ample opportunity to explore it in connection with the speeches the comforters make later on. I want to return to the question that led us to

2:11–13 in the first place: namely, that of how Job "finds himself" put to the test – or more precisely, of our author's first depiction of his suffering protagonist's psychological disposition. You would expect the decisive evidence here to come from Job's own mouth. But, as you saw above, the first three statements he makes – at 1:21 ("the Lord gave, and the Lord has taken away"), at 2:10 ("Shall we receive good at the hand of God, and shall we not receive evil?"), and at 3:3 ("Let the day perish wherein I was born") – give us an apparently contradictory mix of proto-Stoicism and existential nihilism difficult to reconcile in a single character. I want to suggest to you now, having reflected at least provisionally on the structure of the text as a whole and on the role of our weight-bearing transitional passage in particular, that these statements are subject to, governed by, the same discursive gravity as the correspondences, plans, and lamentations of Eliphaz, Bildad, and Zophar. That is, I want to suggest that Job's words, too, bear down on – are drawn into the orbit of – the telling silence reported at 2:13; that his words, too, acquire their direction and weight – their genuine meaning – as a result of its density. Most importantly, I want to suggest that, to the extent that we let this density register on us as readers, we see, in the work of the text itself, a revelation and a reframing of the barren logical contradiction looming in Job's statements as the living existential contradiction of suffering itself – the absolutely central phenomenon that subsequent dialogue then turns around for us until we've seen it from all sides. How might we develop these suggestions?

AN EXERCISE IN ACTING

Come back with me to the possibility of staging the Book of Job – the unintended prompt of my old friend's claim that "we find ourselves put to the test." Imagine yourself cast in the role of our protagonist. A few hours ago, you did a preliminary reading of the adaptation with the full cast. It was difficult. You couldn't seem to find Job's voice, his emotional register. One moment you had to be as serene as Epictetus, the next as desperately pessimistic as Conrad's Mr Kurtz. You know that, unless you can hold these things together, your performance won't be convincing. You've seen plenty of actors deliver dialogue without comprehending and/or expressing the unity of the character they're supposed to inhabit, and it's never good. Now, having had supper, you sit down with the script and a glass of wine to ponder, without the immediate pressure of performance, how you might put your role together.

You recall that, in the reading, the line lifted from 3:3 had given you the greatest trouble. You had said it forcefully, with the edge and bitterness the actual words seem to demand: "Let the day perish wherein I was born." But something seemed to ring false. Along with the actors playing Eliphaz, Bildad, and Zophar you had observed an awkward fifteen seconds of silence in accordance with the rather vague stage direction describing the seven days and nights of wordless communion (the director had made a point of putting its theatrical representation on his "to do" list in the notes he gave at the end of the session). Then you had popped like a cork, fretting at once that you'd wandered against your better judgment into that dubious fraternity of actors who substitute the force of their own unfocused energy for the objective requirements of real performance.

Sipping your wine, you turn the scene around again in your mind. It occurs to you, trying to imagine what your director might do with the passage of time between your second and third interventions, that part of your problem in the reading was precisely that the silence preceding your self-renunciation didn't *mean* anything – or at least didn't mean what it *ought*. Your words don't simply interrupt an awkward pause, they mark the limit, the extremity, of a persistence in suffering your audience needs already to have found remarkable – a persistence you must announce somehow in the proto-Stoicism of your first two lines, then demonstrate even more forcefully in the wordless scene that follows. You tell yourself that you must make this persistence *arise* in your text, even as the words themselves *plunge* into nihilism; that you must embody for your audience the difference between what Job *says* and what he *is*.

Then you are struck by an epiphany: in that difference harbours precisely the dramatic irony you must embody for the
duration of the argument to come. Were you to play our protagonist as merely surrendering to nihilism at 3:3, the ensuing
dialogue, in which he persists, like Socrates, until his interlocutors are driven to silence, would be utterly disingenuous. A real
nihilist – if there is such a thing – *would* simply "curse God and
die." The script, then, both early and late, requires of you something far more subtle than thoroughgoing bitterness. The bitterness you represent must read as the outside of a Stoic endurance.
That endurance must *speak* in your self-renunciation. Or again:
your delivery of the words "let the day perish wherein I was
born" must bear down upon – must be *saturated* by – the silence
that precedes it. You search your memory for some template
appropriate to such a discursive experience. In what kinds of
situations have you encountered a renunciation which is actually
a stage of endurance? Is it like a love affair ended in words but
not in the heart? You won't sort this in the next ten minutes. But
in the meantime, your challenge as an actor has become clearer:
you must draw the line at 3:3 back into the orbit of the telling
silence at 2:13, invest it with the weight of what is unspoken
there, and so perform the existential contradiction of persistence/
renunciation that now appears necessary to the genuine representation of suffering.

Encouraged by the promise of this insight, you turn back to the
lines taken from 1:21 and 2:10. At the reading, you had been
more or less satisfied with their delivery – deliberately calm and
reserved. You had even attempted a hint of whimsy in response to
your wife's injunction to bring down the curtain, hoping to suggest both a higher understanding of your circumstances and a
deeper generosity of spirit. Now though, these choices seem wor-
ryingly flat and static. If 3:3 requires you to communicate an existential state that simultaneously rises and falls, if that state indeed
harbours a dramatic irony, the exploration of which animates the
argument to come, then perhaps the integrity of your character is
inseparable from it. Perhaps Job expresses a kind of psychological antinomy in every word he utters. Mulling this over, your eye

falls on the stage direction just prior to 1:21, which describes Job's initial reaction to the rapid-fire series of bulletins announcing the loss of children and possessions (it had been read but not blocked in the afternoon session): "Then Job arose, and rent his robe, and shaved his head, and fell upon the ground and worshipped" (1:20).

Again, a light comes on. Your being Job – your compression of his character into a single, unified, dramatic gesture – requires the discursive complexity of your first two lines to mirror that of your third. Whereas at 3:3 the long silence of the transitional passage rises into view in the form of persistence as the spoken words plunge, at 1:21 and 2:10 it must *pour out* of the spoken word's lofty height as the despair of a sudden and radical abandonment. Your task as an actor at 3:3 is to portray a bitterness saturated by the unspoken existential contradiction already established at 2:13. At 1:21 and 2:10, it is to present a Stoicism *pregnant* with that contradiction. Here, as before, you search your memory for some appropriate template or guide. In what kinds of situations have you encountered an endurance that is actually the front end of renunciation? Is it like the premonition of disenchantment with a person or principle you've been called upon publicly to defend (surveying my own past, I think of being mandated to win things in a labour negotiation that I began to regard, after long and fruitless battle, as neither necessary nor beneficial)? Time will tell. In the interim, you resolve to try to project your opening lines into the orbit of the telling silence at 2:13, investing them with the weight of what is unspoken there, and so making everything in your opening scene bear down on a single, central contradiction.

The challenges you face in "finding Job" theatrically are not identical with those that emerge for us in the philosophical discussion of his "finding himself." But there is a decisive shared variance: For both actors and philosophical readers, the goal is to bring the text to life. And for both, that liveliness or vitality is made evident in effective representation of a kind of literary integrity. In the widest sense, this integrity is a property of narratives. But when, as with so much of ancient poetry and literature, these narratives unfold in the dialogue of specific individuals, we must come to terms with their integrity as well. "We must," I say, as if reflection on the literary integrity of Job's character were a kind obstacle that had to be circumvented on the way to analysis or description of something else. In fact, it brings us back precisely to representation of the "self" Job "finds" in suffering. And here, in broad strokes at least, what makes sense dramatically is exactly what we're looking for philosophically. The "self" Job "finds" in being put to the test, the "self" that resounds (plunging, arising) in his interventions at 1:21, 2:10, and 3:3 – indeed, as I hope to show, in the whole of the long argument that follows – is the existential contradiction (persistence/renunciation) that first becomes explicit and ultimately comes to rest in the telling silence of our transitional passage.

Finally, and in preparation for looking at the speeches that fill out what scholars call the first cycle of the argument, I should make explicit one way in which actors and philosophers differ as readers, especially since it is germane to the question of grasping the psychological disposition our author wants to represent in the words and deeds of his protagonist. As an actor, you won't be particularly troubled by the prospect of bringing the contradictions of Job's dialogue to life. Virtually all the great characters of the dramatic canon are driven by internal tensions of some kind, and you will have seen what you need to show your audience in your own behaviour or in the behaviour of others in any case. As a philosopher, on the other hand, your detective work – even at this comparatively preliminary stage of our reading – will have brought you to the famously unwieldy phenomenon of language.

How much of its complexity, of its sovereign mystery, is already on display in the simple statements Job makes at 1:21 ("the Lord gave and the Lord has taken away"), 2:10 ("Shall we receive good at the hand of God, and shall we not receive evil?") and 3:3 ("Let the day perish wherein I was born")? His words simultaneously reveal and conceal. They attest in a single gesture both the destruction of all human refuge and the accommodation of all human striving (*conatus*). As self-sufficient assertions, they constitute an outward-facing façade encircling the silent vigil reported at 2:13, doubling and reversing the terms of its governing existential contradiction, constituting in that very play what I called earlier the dramatic irony of Job's character. The philosophical reader must make sense of this complexity, a truly daunting task. We can only hope that the text itself will help us, that our author, master of the fecundity of the word, will in reaping its harvests also show us something of its true nature.

3

Job's Friends Try to Comfort Him

THE WORK OF DRAMATIC IRONY

Among the benefits that accrue from imagining the Book of Job onstage, none surpasses in value the reminder that your task as a reader is to bring your text to life. The challenge of understanding the representation of someone who is living through the kind of misfortune that befalls Job is entirely different from that of understanding a thesis on, or explanation of, suffering for which he is merely a cipher. Your standard working toward the latter is the logic of instrumental reason, in terms of which, as I tried to show in the previous chapter, our protagonist's first three utterances are already problematic. On the way to the former, you're bound to recover features of embodied speech which, though constituting the very element of our daily lives, become oddly inconspicuous in intellectual or scholarly work: the fact that words spoken almost always simultaneously reveal and conceal; that silence may be as or more telling than propositions and arguments; that even an assessment of experience that is, as it were, theologically accurate ("the Lord gave, and the Lord has taken away") or an honest expression of inward turmoil ("let the day perish wherein I was born") may reverse what is true of its object.

In terms of such features, as I've now suggested, Job's position at the outset of the dispute that will challenge and eventually undo the compassion of his friends becomes transparent. Attempting to express the constituents of the contradiction housed somehow in the shared silence reported at 2:13 – destruction of the refuges of personal history and universality, endurance in the striving of *conatus* – he builds a kind of façade around it that threatens to obscure it entirely. His words flatten and falsify the experience of what we might call his sufferer's integrity. For you, the sympathetic reader, he presents the tremendously sad spectacle of someone whose pain has pushed him to the brink of self-abnegation. At the same time, the very things he fails to represent are perceptible to you as *moving in him*. The loss of refuge pours out of his stoicism, the endurance of *conatus* rises from his nihilism. The very stasis of his spoken words frames for you a more fundamental dynamism that, although hidden from Job himself, actually constitutes the integrity of his being. How will you make sense of this?

You might begin by recalling that the comedies and tragedies of Western literature show us regularly the disjunction between the self-expression of characters and the deeper integrities of their being. Take, for example, Shakespeare's *Twelfth Night*. In one famous, very funny scene, we see Olivia's steward Malvolio strolling in the courtyard of the estate. He finds a letter he takes to be hers, planted in plain view by the real authors – Sir Toby, Sir Andrew, and the maid, Maria. As they watch, stifling giggles and insults, he reads their work aloud, walking sentence by sentence toward the deluded conclusion that his mistress secretly loves him, toward the conviction that his destiny is to be the master of her house, not servant in it. As the scene closes, he speaks his mind directly to the audience:

Daylight and champagne discovers not more! This is open.
I will be proud, I will read politic authors, I will baffle
Sir Toby, I will wash off gross acquaintance, I will be point-
devise the very man. I do not now fool myself, to let imagination jade me; for every reason excites to this, that my lady
loves me.[1]

The comedy here is achieved precisely in the representation of Malvolio's not knowing who he is. The letter written by his tormentors is a kind of riddle, the solution to which must be provided by the distortion of his self-aggrandizement. What he reveals to the audience in the passage above, in a spirit of triumph and self-congratulation, is his almost limitless capacity for self-deception. As with Job, then, the stasis of the spoken word in Shakespeare's comedy may frame the dynamism of something unspoken. You appreciate the humour of the courtyard scene because – like Toby, Andrew, and Maria – you see Malvolio's self-deception pouring out of his pride.

But you might look as well at Sophocles' *Oedipus Rex*, the veritable paradigm of the tragic form. In its magisterial overture, the king finds supplicants on the steps of his palace. The city has been afflicted by plagues. In desperation, its citizens, young and old, have come to their sovereign for help. Oedipus, as it turns out, has already sent his emissary, Creon, to the Pythian house of Apollo to learn from the seers there what measures of purification might be required. Mid-scene, Creon returns with the diagnosis: Thebes is suffering because the murderer of its previous king, Laius, remains unpunished. The problem is that no one knows his identity. For the sake of his people, Oedipus vows to solve this mystery. He says to Creon:

> I will start afresh; and bring everything into the light. All
> praise to Phoebus – and thanks to you – for pointing out our
> duty to the dead. You will find me as willing an ally as you
> could wish in the cause of God and our country. My own
> cause too – not merely from a fellow-creature will I clear this
> taint, but from myself. The killer of Laius, whoever he was,
> might think to turn his hand against *me*; thus, serving Laius,
> I serve myself.[2]

These words are entirely appropriate, given what Oedipus knows as the play opens. But you hear in them also the countermovement of its complete narrative arc – and that countermovement effectively reverses the meaning of his pledges to Creon. He *will* "bring everything to light," but not in the way he imagines. He *will* "clear this taint" from the city and from himself, but not by

sniffing out a hidden assassin. He *will* serve himself in the end –
inasmuch as he endures in the definitively human quest for truth
– but only at the cost of his position, his reputation, his health,
and his personal happiness. As with Malvolio, what you see
in Oedipus is a character deceived. But the effect is different.
Watching Shakespeare's drama unfold, you presume the pomp-
ous steward will suffer because of his own foolishness. Oedipus,
on the other hand, will fall because he aspires to what is best in
human life: protecting his community, honouring the gods and
the dead, understanding the causes of things. In the passage
above, Sophocles shows you the inevitable tide of ruin already
rising in the promise of justice. It floods (and so destabilizes) the
calm of the king's spoken reassurance.

In the sense that Job's words, too, draw attention to the uncanny
capacity of language for movement in stasis, you may plot him on
the spectrum of literary characters, comic and tragic, whose interventions develop and/or reveal the larger designs – the deeper
messages – of dramatic irony. At the same time, though, you can
distinguish Job from the Malvolios and Oedipuses of the Western
tradition in a way that makes the design of his story, its narrative
arc or architecture, more accessible. In contrast to the comic
dupe, his misfortune is clearly undeserved. Nothing in his character warrants it. And where, more often than not, the fool's undoing culminates in recrimination of some kind – in the unambiguous
demonstration of his failure to learn (Malvolio's last words: "I'll
be revenged on the whole pack of you"[3]) – Job's odyssey ends in
epiphany and transformation (42:5–6: "I had heard of thee by
the hearing of the ear, but now my eye sees thee; therefore I
despise myself, and repent in dust and ashes"). In contrast to the
tragic hero, Job's ruin comes early. His losses are fully recorded in
the opening scene. Indeed, where more often than not you find
the hero utterly alone, in exile, or dead by the time the final curtain comes down ("Go then," Creon says to the blinded Oedipus
in their final exchange, "but leave the children"[4]), the end of the
Book of Job shows you a flourish of divine generosity that undoes
– at least materially – the damage incurred by the original wager
with Satan (42:10, 16: "and the Lord gave Job twice as much as

he had before ... and after this Job lived a hundred and forty years, and saw his sons, and his sons' sons, four generations"). Or again, where the terminus of tragic irony is almost always a scene of devastation, the movement in stasis of the Biblical poetry brings us, in the end, to a spiritual (and physical) restoration.

In advance of working through the materials of the dialogue – that is, the moral/theological propositions of Job's comforters and the series of his own rejoinders, Elihu's exasperated interruptions, God's sermons of fury and love – take a moment to read this outcome explicitly in terms of the transition from poetry to prose at 2:11–13. That text again:

> Now when Job's three friends heard of all this evil that
> had come upon him, they came each from his own place,
> Eliphaz the Temanite, Bildad the Shuhite, and Zophar the
> Na'amathite. They made an appointment together to come to
> condole with him and comfort him. And when they saw him
> from afar, they did not recognize him; and they rent their
> robes and sprinkled dust upon their heads toward heaven.
> And they sat with him on the ground seven days and seven
> nights, and no one spoke a word to him, for they saw that his
> suffering was very great.

If what I said about the structural role of these verses in the preceding chapter is right, if they offer a kind of contact point that bears the weight of the entire text, then there will be a sense in which even the event of Job's restoration pushes back toward his original silence. And that means, in turn, that the play of discourses constituting this event – the arguments of Chapters 3 to 41, which to all appearances efface or transcend the original wordless communion of Job, Eliphaz, Bildad, and Zophar – must lead us, by movement in stasis of one form or another, *back* to it. Here then is a hypothesis for reading the Book of Job: what you need to grasp above all in weighing its message is the work of its dramatic irony. Our author wants to turn the reductive façade of language against itself in order precisely to recuperate the sufferer's integrity that it conceals. Although this work has all the art of a Derridian deconstruction, it is no mere display of cleverness. On the contrary, the description of suffering requires an account of its moral and theological misrepresentations. And that is because to surmount the kind of pain Job experiences means, among other things, to surmount these misrepresentations, to see them undone in others and in ourselves. To put the point as bluntly as possible: you need to grasp the work of the Book of Job's dramatic irony because it is the irony of life itself.

How then do you apprehend the words of Job's comforters in terms of the movement in stasis already at play in the first three utterances, that is, in terms of the text's framing irony? At a minimum, it seems to me, you need to make sense of three things: the transition from silence to dialogue (3:3–4:2); the specific utility of each character – Eliphaz, Bildad, Zophar – in the articulation of the morality/theology of suffering; and the so-called cycles of that articulation – Chapters 4 to 14, 15 to 21, and 22 to 25 respectively, in which, it seems, the same arguments are repeated in the face of a clearly diminishing return. With respect to each of these items, what you need to see above all is a kind of emotional logic; the scaffolding of a line-by-line commentary you might develop in a closer, more scholarly reading elsewhere. Elaborating this logic, I leave Job's speeches aside, except where reference to them is absolutely necessary. The irony of *his* argument will be the story of the next chapter.

FROM SILENCE TO DIALOGUE

Go back, first, to the cry of anguish at 3:3 – "Let the day perish wherein I was born" – not, this time, to ponder what might be at play in *speaking* these words but to grasp the consequences of *hearing* them. It's not difficult to imagine in more pedestrian circumstances the kind of challenge Job's self-abnegation presents to his friends. Think of the person with whom you've shared a political cause, a project, or an institution, who – for plausible reasons – loses faith in it and tells you so in no uncertain terms. Your position is uncomfortable. On the one hand, you want to acknowledge the loss by standing in solidarity with your colleague ("Yes, the party leadership is hopelessly out of touch," "Yes, our fundraising effort seems doomed to fail," "Yes, the university board has surrendered itself completely to the business model of government bureaucracy"). On the other, you want to protect your own investments. After all, it's also your work and your attempts to make sense of the world (a labour that constitutes, among other things, the ground of your relations with your interlocutor) that now stands under threat. Normally, you try to split the difference by dissolving your colleague's complaints in a more pragmatic, "warts and all" commitment to the enterprise in question ("What political organization isn't called upon, from time to time, to succeed in spite of its leaders?" "What financial campaign, especially in hard times, isn't visited by the spectre of failure?" "What university, the nonsense of its governing bodies notwithstanding, isn't still capable of representing the riches of its intellectual traditions in its classrooms?") This may or may not work. The one option you don't have – at least in honest conversation – is silence. That was acceptable, perhaps even best, as long as the two of you were soldiering on with your work. Once your colleague despairs out loud, it becomes the tacit surrender of your own faith.

Your solidarity, then, must be expressed. And it must aim at recuperating and affirming anew the significance of your shared enterprise. How much more is that the case in the radically non-pedestrian circumstances of the Book of Job, where the enterprise in question is life itself! The cry of anguish at 3:3 is a condemnation of the whole human condition, an indictment of the accommodations of experience that, prior to his misfortune, Job shared with his friends. They must respond to it, or concede the truth of its nihilism. All this is evident in the first verses of Chapter 4, which display both the tenderness of a comforter's solidarity and the resolve to protect the most basic philosophical investments: "Then Eliphaz the Temanite answered: 'If one ventures a word with you, will you be offended? Yet who can keep from speaking?'" You could put the point another way, extending the theme of accommodation I introduced earlier when reflecting both on the philosophies of Heidegger and Plato and on the words of my old friend: Job's cry of anguish denies both himself and his comforters the hospitality of silence. Its negativity effaces the previously evident miracle of his own endurance, imposing on the others the necessity of restoring him, by means of persuasion, to the universal and personal grounds of sense and value. What I called above the specific utility of the characters of Eliphaz, Bildad, and Zophar in the articulation of the morality/theology of suffering needs to be grasped in terms of that persuasion.

ELIPHAZ, BILDAD, AND ZOPHAR

With this in view, look first at Eliphaz. The speech that unfolds on the heels of the rhetorical question above (4:3–5:27) gives you the lynchpin of all subsequent arguments. "Think now," he says:

> who that was innocent ever perished? Or where were the
> upright cut off? As I have seen, those who plow iniquity and
> sow trouble reap the same. By the breath of God they perish,
> and by his anger they are consumed. The roar of the lion,
> the voice of the fierce lion, the teeth of the young lions, are
> broken. The strong lion perishes for lack of prey, and the
> whelps of the lioness are scattered. (4:7–11)

Here you are led back deliberately to the template for the basic intelligibility of the world – to what I called in the first chapter the refuge of universality – in a form specifically tailored for Job: the *cosmos* created and sustained by God rewards the upright and the punishes the wicked. Divine justice obtains regardless of the apparent power of those subject to it (even the lion may be "broken"). Its dominion is without limit, its principle absolutely inviolable. You simply can't overstate the importance of this thesis. Some form of it appears in all subsequent speeches. It is the foundation of the friends' moral/theological position, the first principle of their philosophy of life, and so the explicit ground of their comfort. If Job now renounces the very day of his birth, taking this view, it's because his present suffering has shaken out of him the long-standing (and justifiable) conviction that an "upright" man will always be at home in God's world. And if that's the case, the challenge of consoling him is clear: Job must be led back to accommodation in the order of rewards and punishments.

Undertaking this work, Eliphaz begins by reminding his friend that prior to his own misfortunes he himself had consoled others regularly, engaging in advocacy of the very theological position his cry of anguish now forces his friends to reiterate and defend:

> Behold you have instructed many, and you have strengthened weak hands. Your words have upheld him who was stumbling and you have made firm the feeble knees. But now it has come to you, and you are impatient; it touches you and you are dismayed. Is not your fear of God your confidence, and the integrity of your ways your hope? (4:3–6)

It's a powerful point. Job has thrown out faith in God's justice as a lifeline to others. With what right does he refuse it himself? And yet, as becomes abundantly clear in subsequent dialogue, the "integrity" that makes Job an ideal candidate for the kind of consolation he's provided in the past is also a potentially devastating obstacle to his accepting it at present. That is because the hope of someone genuinely "upright," in terms of the straightforward moral theology Eliphaz articulates at 4:7–11, is dashed in suffering as such. What I mean is: the suffering of the upright (the "blameless") is itself proof that human righteousness offers insufficient protection against punishment. Someone in Job's situation might hang on to the thought that God doles out rewards and punishments (compare again his response to his wife at 2:10), but not that the origin of such things is anything like warranted. The absence of warrant, however, appears to reduce the assignment of fates to chance – giving Job (and, by extension, you and I) nothing to ward off despair when his "luck" runs out.

Eliphaz knows this. Failure to address the question of how someone like his friend – to all appearances upright and blameless – might warrant his afflictions threatens his theological position with incoherence. That is why, at 4:12, he turns from what you might call the facts of experience, where the measure of divine justice seems in the case at hand problematic, to the authority of dream-vision or epiphany, where forces greater than human observation offer us the possibility of a deeper understanding:

> Now a word was brought to me stealthily, my ear received whisper of it. Amid thoughts from visions of the night, when deep sleep falls on men, dread came upon me, and trembling, which made all my bones shake. A spirit glided past my face: the hair of my flesh stood up. It stood still but I could not discern its appearance. A form was before my eyes; there was silence, then I heard a voice: "Can mortal man be righteous before God? Can a man be pure before his Maker? Even in his servants he puts no trust, and his angels he charges with error; how much more those who dwell in houses of clay, whose foundation is in the dust, who are crushed before the moth. Between morning and evening they are destroyed; they persist for ever without any regarding it. If their tent-cord is plucked up within them, do they not die, and that without wisdom?" (4:12–21)

The vision effectively commutes the thesis of 4:7–11 to human nature itself. God rewards the upright and punishes the wicked. But all of us *as mortals* "plow iniquity and sow trouble" in some measure. Finite or created being as such is impure. There's a great song from Bob Dylan's gospel period, "What Can I Do for You?" that riffs on the thought Eliphaz develops here: "Soon as a man is born you know the sparks begin to fly. He gets wise in his own eyes and is made to believe a lie."[5] (Compare 5:6–7: "For affliction does not come from the dust, nor does trouble sprout from the ground, but man is born to trouble as the sparks fly upward.") Human beings may – indeed, must – strive toward righteousness, but as mortal, finite, created beings they will fail to perfect it. Accordingly, no one is safe from punishment and everyone stands in need of deliverance ("As for me, I would seek God, and to God would I commit my cause," 5:8). The real function of misfortune, especially if, to all appearances, it arrives out of the blue, is to remind you of this. But that means in turn that nihilism of the kind Job expresses at 3:3 is evidence of a dangerous hubris ("Surely vexation kills the fool," 5:2). Instead of despairing, he ought to retrace the path of insight now broken by his friend, from the ethical order of rewards and punishments by and large visible in experience to the natural limits of human integrity revealed in the vision. In that context, even Job's suffering is comprehensible: the refuge of universality is restored.

For my purposes, two things bear notice in the "Job" chapters that separate Eliphaz's speech (4:1–5:27) from Bildad's (8:1–22). First, the former's mix of tenderness and pious theological resolve elicits from our protagonist a qualified retraction of his outburst at 3:3. "O that my vexation were weighed, and all my calamity laid in the balances!" he begins, "For then it would be heavier than the sand of the sea: therefore my words have been rash" (6:2–3). Some gesture of this kind is indispensable to the success of Eliphaz's intervention. If Job remains resolutely nihilistic, the conversation is over before it begins. But – and this would be the second point – Job's engagement of Eliphaz's theology comes with the inevitable question about *his* place in it. He sees immediately the price of accepting his friend's argument: his suffering *makes sense* as punishment. It's steep and difficult to comprehend: "Teach me and I will be silent," he says simply at 6:24, "make me understand how I have erred." The challenge is clear. If the comfort held out by Job's friends is to restore the world that has unravelled in his suffering, something more than the "cunning cloud" of the universal is necessary.[6] The reduction of suffering to punishment must be made concrete. Or again: rescue from despair requires more than theological abstraction. Its narrative must incorporate the sufferer explicitly.

This is the work of Bildad and Zophar, the proverbial "bad cops" were you to imagine the Book of Job on the model of a police interrogation. Bildad's angle is guilt by association. Job may be reaping the whirlwind stirred up by those close to him. To the extent that his comfort amounts to a tacit sanction of their offences, it will have been sacrificed in order to set all things right:

Does God pervert justice? Or does the Almighty pervert
the right? If your children have sinned against him, he has
delivered them into the power of their transgression. If you will
seek God and make supplication to the Almighty, if you are
pure and upright, surely then he will rouse himself for you and
reward you with a rightful habitation. And though your beginning was small your latter days will be very great. (8:3–7)

When, without acknowledging the sins of his children, Job takes
offence at this ("It is all one … he destroys both the blameless
and the wicked," 9:22), it becomes evident to this interlocutors
that he cannot be spared the direct expression of the conclusion
that follows from Eliphaz's premises. Zophar delivers it at the
outset of his speech, without tact or tenderness:

Should a multitude of words go unanswered, and a man full
of talk be vindicated? Should your babble silence men, and
when you mock, shall no one shame you? For you say, "My
doctrine is pure, and I am clean in God's eyes." But, oh, that
God would speak, and open his lips to you, and that he would
tell you the secrets of wisdom! For he is manifold in understanding. Know then that God exacts of you less than *your
guilt* deserves. (11:2–6, italics mine)

Draw back here a moment. You're now within hailing distance
of a hypothesis on the roles of Eliphaz, Bildad, and Zophar. You
may conceive their work at this point in terms of two comple-
mentary developments. The first is unidirectional, deductive: in the
service of elaborating the moral theology introduced at 4:7–11,
Job's friends fill out the author's narrative the way propositions
fill out an argument. Each has, as it were, his logical function.
Eliphaz stands to Bildad and Zophar as the major premise of the
traditional Aristotelian syllogism stands to its minor premise and
its conclusion. To paraphrase for the sake of formal clarity:

ELIPHAZ: In God's world, reward follows virtue, punishment/
suffering follows vice.

BILDAD/ZOPHAR: Job and his household are at present being punished/suffering.

BILDAD/ZOPHAR: Therefore, Job and his household must have been guilty of vice.

At the same time this syllogistic division of labour makes evident a shift in the way the friends as a collective *reach out* to Job in his suffering. Each articulates, as it were, a station of this reversal. And while its contour is dictated by the logical inference, its eventual point of rest is not, on that account, any less perplexing. The fact is that what begins sincerely and tentatively as comfort, to the surprise of the reader and the disappointment of Job himself, ends in unequivocal judgment:

ELIPHAZ: "If one ventures a word with you, will you be offended?"

BILDAD: "If your children sinned against him, he has delivered them into the power of their transgression."

ZOPHAR: "Know then that God exacts of you less than your guilt deserves."

The number of comforters, then, and the manner in which our author draws them, serves both the argument and the intentionality of the Book of Job's first cycle. But coming back now directly to my hypothesis for reading, these things, taken together, constitute another instance of the movement in stasis I described above, drawing on scenes from comedy and tragedy. The (moral/theogical) syllogism is the reductive facade of language (the equivalent of Malvolio's decoding Olivia's desire, or of Oedipus's vowing to avenge Laius), the shift in allegiance (pro-Job – anti-Job) the counter-subject that, once played, reveals its inadequacy. What we need to ponder is whether and how the dramatic irony of the friends' speeches might also repeat and extend the gravitational effect you discovered in the statements at 1:21 and 2:10 when you imagined them on stage. Or again: whether and how there might be a unified philosophic vision expressed in the prologue and the first cycle of the dialogue.

COLD COMFORT – IDEOLOGY AND RAGE

We could come at this (conveniently) by thinking a little about the final item on our present agenda: the purpose of the dialogue's multiple cycles. Here, as before, I put aside scholarly comment. The idea of adding something meaningful to the secondary literature on the Book of Job – to the 2,000-plus-year tradition of detailed textual exegesis – ought to fill even the most prodigiously talented students of the Hebrew Scriptures with dread (never mind someone with my journeyman's skills). Instead, repeat with me the experience we can speak to with confidence, the naive encounter of the text. It seems to me very likely that, however esoteric and ingenious the details of his composition, our author must also have had people like me in mind – non-expert readers looking for help on the questions of life, looking *through* the story at the sovereign mysteries of accommodation and abandonment, rationality and nihilism, suffering and healing. What do such readers take from the cycles of argument (Chapters 4 to 31)?

Looking back on my own experiences, I would point to three things. First, taking up in more detail now an earlier remark, the theology of reward and punishment introduced by Eliphaz at 4:7–8 returns with what a colleague of mine once called (in another context) "punishing regularity." He comes back to it, for example, in his contribution to the second cycle:

> I will show you, hear me; and what I have seen I will declare (what wise men have told, and their fathers have not hidden, to whom alone the land was given, and no stranger passed among them). The wicked man writhes in pain all his days, through all the years that are laid up for the ruthless. Terrifying sounds are in his ears; in prosperity the destroyer will come upon him. (15:17–21)

And again, at the end of his final intervention:

> For God abases the proud but he saves the lowly. He delivers the innocent man; you will be delivered through the cleanness of your hands. (22:29–30)

Bildad's first counsel – the speech that begins by hypothesizing the guilt of Job's children – concludes:

> Behold, God will not reject a blameless man, nor take the hand of evildoers. He will yet fill your mouth with laughter and your lips with shouting. Those who hate you will be clothed with shame, and the tent of the wicked will be no more. (8:20–22)

His second, in Chapter 18, is essentially a litany of punishments reserved for the wicked. It reads in part:

> Yea, the light of the wicked is put out, and the flame of his fire does not shine. The light is dark in his tent, and his lamp above him is put out ... His roots dry up beneath and his branches wither above. His memory perishes from the earth, and he has no name in the street. He is thrust from light into darkness and driven out of the world. He has no offspring or descendant among his people, and no survivor where he used to live. They of the west are appalled at his day, and horror seizes them at the east. Surely such are the dwellings of the ungodly, such is the place of him who knows not God. (18:5–6, 16–21)

And Zophar? His chastisement of Job in the speech of the first cycle – the proverbial conclusion of the friends' syllogism – eventually recuperates the major premise:

> If you set your heart aright, you will stretch out your hands toward him. If iniquity is in your hand, put it far away, and let not wickedness dwell in your tents. Surely then you will lift up your face without blemish; you will be secure, and will not fear ... But the eyes of the wicked will fail; all way of escape will be lost to them, and their hope is to breathe their last. (11:13–5, 20)

Then his final words, in Chapter 20, which extend and intensify the "fire and brimstone" of his colleagues:

Do you not know this from of old, since man was placed
upon the earth that the exulting of the wicked is short, and
the joy of the godless but for a moment? Though his height
mount up to the heavens, and his head reach to the clouds,
he will perish forever like his own dung; those who have seen
him will say, "Where is he?" He will fly away like a dream,
and not be found; he will be chased away like a vision of the
night. The eye which saw him will see him no more, nor will
his place any more behold him. His children will seek the
favour of the poor, and his hands will give back his wealth.
His bones are full of youthful vigour but it will lie down
with him in the dust ... The possessions of his house will be
carried away, dragged off in the day of God's wrath. This is
the wicked man's portion from God, the heritage decreed for
him by God. (20:4–11, 28–9)

I'll be blunt here. I found the force of the argument in these
passages inversely proportional to the number of its iterations. It
seemed to me reasonable enough at 4:7–11 as a counter to Job's
nihilism. But by the time the punishments of the wicked were
reprised at 20:4, the friends had become to my ear the kinds of
boors who dominate political conventions, news channels, and
blogospheres, talking heads who stay on message no matter what
they are asked. The thesis that struck me in Eliphaz's first speech
as a sincere and responsive attempt at comfort I saw degrade,
over roughly forty-five minutes of reading, first into something
like an ideology, then into something like rage. I can't believe that
our author, having weighed every phrase of his composition,
would have let this effect seep into it unawares. On the contrary,
it seems to me that he must have set out to represent the diminishing return of the repeated argument as a moment of his description of suffering, and that the cycles of the dialogue – themselves
repetitions of a sort – were designed to serve this representation.

With this in view, notice, secondly, that in the theatre of discussion the friends shore up their position by making it non-
falsifiable. It happens on two fronts. Epistemologically, they
counter Job's insistence on the evident fact of his integrity with

the claim that the ultimate ground of such things is non-evident, that individuals are incapable of evaluating their own moral status, that the ways of God (though always just) are inscrutable to reason. Implicit here, interestingly, is an argument for Job's guilt that requires neither knowledge nor judgment of his life prior to the catastrophes of his suffering. If "the fear of the Lord is the beginning of wisdom" (Proverbs 1:7), his objections themselves are evidence of a foolish impiety. Look again at Zophar's syllogism-clinching charge at the end of the first cycle. It already states this case provisionally: "For you say: 'My doctrine is pure, and I am clean in God's eyes.' But oh that God would speak, and open his lips to you, and that he would tell you the secrets of his wisdom! For he is manifold in understanding."

Eliphaz expands the indictment in the first speech of the second cycle – framing the problem explicitly in terms of "the fear of God" and the limits of human knowledge:

> But you are doing away with the fear of God, and hindering meditation before God, for your iniquity teaches your mouth, and you choose the tongue of the crafty ... Are you the first man that was born? Or were you brought forth before the hills? Have you listened in the council of God? And do you limit wisdom to yourself?

And at the beginning of the third cycle he asks – rhetorically, I think, in order to keep before us the precise nature of what he takes to be Job's hubris: "Is it for your fear of (God) that he reproves you, and enters into judgment with you?"

The epistemological claim is bolstered by the assessment of mortal life I tagged earlier reviewing the introduction of the theology of reward and punishment in Chapter 4. As it turns out, Job lacks not only the intellectual capacity to evaluate his situation; the state of innocence he claims is actually beyond his *nature*. "Man," Eliphaz says, "is *born* to trouble" (5:7, italics mine). In the final words our author allots to the comforters, Bildad reprises this point in a kind of reverse benediction – as if to seal off definitively, the possibility of further objections: "How then can man be righteous before God? How can he who is born of woman be clean? Behold, even the moon is not bright and the stars are not clean in his sight; how much less man who is a maggot, and the son of man who is a worm!" (25:4–6).

Denial of the very possibility of objections, of recalcitrant cases, seems to me a principal trait of ideologies. In contrast to the responsive attitude motivated precisely by a wonder that opens things up, ideologues look to close things down, to articulate a principle or set of principles that settles questions definitively. This attitude no doubt takes itself to be working in defence of what I've been calling the refuge of universality. And, in a certain way, anyone striving to understand the world needs to anticipate or imagine what a definitive account of it might look like. But, as "the slaughter-bench of history"7 attests, the price of imposing such an account, whether by reifying it in a political regime or insisting on it in personal relations, is intolerably high. It reduces counter-evidence – the very thing genuine thought must engage creatively – to irrationality. And where the presentation of counter-evidence persists, as it does in Job's discourses, the ideologue will perceive in it an offence against reason, a kind of destructive nonsense.

As a result, notice, thirdly, that the friends' *in*flation of the theology of reward and punishment unfolds in lockstep with a polemical *de*flation of Job's counter-arguments, that is, with an attempt to portray his objections – even his questions – as the nattering of a windbag. Indeed, in a remarkable bit of compositional symmetry, our author has Eliphaz, Bildad, and Zophar deplore Job's incoherence in the second verse of four consecutive speeches in the first and second cycles:

BILDAD (1st cycle): How long will you say these things and the words of your mouth be a great wind? (8:2)
ZOPHAR (1st cycle): Should a multitude of words go unanswered and a man full of talk be vindicated? (11:2)
ELIPHAZ (2nd cycle): Should a wise man answer with windy knowledge, and fill himself with the east wind? (15:2)
BILDAD (2nd cycle): How long will you hunt for words? Consider, and then we will speak. (18.2)

Here something more than ideology plays out. In these passages, the respect required for dialogue has disappeared entirely.
Job's interlocutors strip him of the dignity of speech. They claim
on behalf of their argument alone the mantle of rationality. To the
extent that this claim takes hold, the discussion is no longer mediated by reason. On the contrary, it becomes the unmediated rage
of reason against its opposite. And although the litanies of reward
and punishment continue beyond 18:2, my own sense was that
the friends' response to Job's suffering culminates in rage; that
their final purpose was to annul the possibility of meaningful
resistance. It would be too easy, and indefensible even on a cur-
sory reading of the text, to argue that this devolution – first from
responsiveness to ideology, then from ideology to rage – con-
forms as neatly to the three cycles of the argument (Chapters 4 to
25) as the friends themselves (in Chapters 4 to 11) to the stations
of the Aristotelian syllogism. But those cycles, taken as a whole,
nevertheless articulate and accommodate the logic of the descent.

Where are we, then? At the beginning of this chapter, I suggested to you that what we need to grasp above all in weighing
the message of the Book of Job is the work of its dramatic irony,
that our author wants to turn the reductive façade of language
against itself in order precisely to recuperate the sufferer's integrity it conceals. You see an epitome of this work in the drama of
Job's interventions at 1:21, 2:10, and 3:3. Inhabiting his words,
imagining them as an actor – as someone charged with the
responsibility of bringing them to life – you apprehend the despair
pouring out of his stoicism, the endurance rising from his nihilism. But now look! What the friends give you, arguably, is a
detailed pathology of the first of these movements. In the diaboli-
cal syllogism of the first cycle, assurance dispenses judgment. In
the repetitions of the theology of reward and punishment that
resound in the second and third cycles, responsive understanding
dispenses ideological rage. In both cases, our author, at once
stage-managing his play and exposing its illusions, seems to say:
"Follow me around back of human reason – around back of stoicism, assurance, and responsive understanding. Just offstage,
holding up its façade, we find the opposite! Reason is really the

vessel of despair, of unforgiving condemnation, of rage. You think not? Watch: I'll show you how these things pour out!"

It's more than enough to cause a journeyman philosopher anxiety. If the friends' argument devolves in anything like the way I've suggested, if my experience captures anything like our author's intent, then the balm for Job's nihilism, the very thing that is supposed to restore to him the refuge of universality, constitutes its undoing, its destruction. And that means in turn: human reason does not reduce suffering. By its means, rather, the sufferer's homelessness is elevated to the status of an ineluctable necessity. Is it any wonder Job and his friends kept silence seven days and nights? Any wonder the shattering of that silence was an irrational cry of despair? If our reason undoes its own attempts at accommodation, what possibility is there of avoiding abandonment?

4

Job Is Patient

Henry Bugbee was the teacher of my teacher, an association that conferred on him, at least for me, the status of philosophical patriarch or grandfather. I met him only once, very briefly. He came, post-retirement, to my alma mater the year after I left for graduate school. I was there, by chance, at the time, prowling old haunts on my winter break. On the Friday afternoon of that week in late February, sunny and already pregnant with spring, faculty, senior students, and one or two hangers-on like me gathered in the converted living room of the old place that housed the Philosophy Department in those days to hear our guest talk about the *Iliad*. More than thirty years on, the contents of his lecture have faded from memory. What remains, surprisingly vivid, is the impression of what might best be called his *bearing*, which was somehow tremendously austere and kind at once. Above all: serious. I remember thinking that the sort of banter I'd heard in past colloquia, where participants found in the speaker's presentation an occasion for promoting their contending intellectual alliances, was here completely out of place, like gossip in the celebration of a sacred rite. Bugbee presented to us an intellectual dignity that made customary academic behaviour seem shamefully derivative. I kept my own trap firmly shut.

Years later, on the job as a novice professor of philosophy, but struggling for my voice as a writer, I thought of that Friday afternoon. It occurred to me that, in spite of his being my grandfather, I hadn't read a word of Bugbee's published work, that I didn't know so much as the title of a book or an essay. Suddenly curious, I went to the library and typed his name into the search engine. Ten minutes later I was reading *The Inward Morning*,[1] his only self-standing monograph. Inside its covers, remarkably, I discovered the same bearing, the same improbable mix of austerity and kindness, the same seriousness, presented this time in the form of an authorship. And there was something else I had failed to notice at the seminar – perhaps because I hadn't really begun to write myself – which seems to me now utterly crucial: the almost paradoxical effect of a voice whose intimate individuality nested in complete surrender to the matter of its thought.

I recall these episodes for two reasons. First: because when we get to Chapter 38 of our story, to the voice from the whirlwind (to what we might well call the apotheosis of suffering), I'm going to solicit Bugbee's aid when considering the question of how we ought to hear it – in which case it will be helpful for you to remember him in something like the way I do. But second, and more idiosyncratically: of late I've been imagining a kind of interview I might conduct with the author of the Book of Job, in which he has the half-remembered face, the posture, and the demeanour of my teacher's teacher. Who knows why? I suppose if you set yourself the task of imagining everyone's philosophical grandfather (what epoch of Western history is untouched by the text you and I are trying to understand?) it's only natural to fasten at least initially on your own. At least then the person for whom we now lack even a name seems potentially knowable, someone I might sit down with (however timidly), whose words and gestures I might picture (however vaguely).

The setting of my imagined interview is a dusty outdoor café somewhere in the countryside of modern Israel. I've never been to the Middle East. The picture I call to mind is pinched from a slide show given by one of my colleagues, featuring shots of an archeological dig she had done with her husband in Jordan.[2] I'm sitting at a table like the one in her photo, under a kind of awning meant to shade patrons from the heat of the midday sun. I see our author approaching. On entering the café's enclosure, he is welcomed by the owner as a regular, a gesture that simultaneously humanizes him while making me feel more the outsider. The two of them converse for about twenty seconds before turning together in my direction. Something in this gesture produces the sudden worry that the space of my reverie is shared somehow, like a webpage: that this scene has had thousands of hits; that the substance of the owner's greeting has been something like, "Sorry, old friend, yet another one here about your book."

I feel a stab of shame. My breezy sketch of the tell-all stage manager at the end of the last chapter doesn't capture the comportment of the person now walking toward me. I might have behaved that way; he wouldn't. Chastened by this thought, I look down at my list of questions: on the the Book of Job's sources and silences, on the specific ironies of the protagonist's first words, on the utility of Eliphaz, Bildad, and Zophar and the cyclic design of their theological argument, on the discursive representation of patience, on the vision of time and imagination in Elihu's chapters, on the Spinoza-friendly message of the voice from the whirlwind, on the nature of restoration and healing – ultimately, on whether a convincing description of suffering can be reconciled with the idea of a world that is welcoming or loving. The agenda's too long! In galloping through it, I'll only call attention to the derivative nature of *my own* labours at the expense of the matter itself. "No!" I think. "Our patriarch deserves something better than the idiosyncratic set pieces of a would-be commentator. I need to rise to the level of real conversation, to do my share of the work involved in the search for wisdom and understanding!"

And so ... having greeted him, introduced myself, and ordered drinks, I decide on the spur of the moment to extemporize on one theme with which I'm already well acquainted. "I grew up on post-Enlightenment European philosophy," I begin. "Late-nineteenth and twentieth centuries. Do you know the era?" He shakes his head almost imperceptibly, but appears to be giving me his full attention. "Its leading lights were engaged, more or less continually, in what you might call an autopsy of instrumental reason." He looks perplexed. "The kind of argument deployed by Eliphaz and company," I add, thinking his issue is the frame of reference appropriate to "reason."

Instead, he says, "Yes, but why an 'autopsy'?"

My metaphor was spontaneous. Now I must develop it. "I suppose," I say hesitantly, "because, for the principal strands of the thinking I have in mind, the substance and method of the Western intellectual tradition appears moribund – like the corpse-host of a parasite." Then I see a way forward: "Karl Marx reduced reason to the vessel of ideology, to expression of the interests of the ruling class; Nietzsche decried it as the husk of slavish Christian decadence, of a world-denying nihilism; Heidegger charged it with concealing the progressive forgetting of Being that culminates in reduction of the world to the status of resource and raw material for the technological will; Foucault uncovered in the processes of its institutionalization a kind of bourgeois rage, a mania for absolute control of knowledge, of sexuality, of discipline and punishment, of vital power. In every case," I continue, driving now more confidently back to my original point, "what seems called for by experience and by the events of the age is a philosophical dissection of what the tradition calls 'reason.' And," I conclude, "in every case the dissection exposes some form of un-reason, of barbarism, of spiritual catastrophe. 'The fully enlightened earth radiates disaster triumphant.'"[3]

There, I think: Some intellectual momentum. Not of my own making certainly – but born, at least, of a world novel and unknown to him. Move to the question! "One of the astounding features of your poem," I continue, "especially given its age, is its anticipation of post-Enlightenment criticism. The main dialogue follows reason to the point where it undoes the very accommodation it promises, to the point where it performs the sufferer's abandonment. You do this not by adopting an external point of view (no one, least of all Job himself, gives up on argument per se) but by providing a phenomenology of the manner in which reason fails itself, the manner in which it shows itself reduced to ideology, ultimately to rage. In other words, you come to the conclusion that enlightenment descends into barbarism simply by framing the operations of reason in the story of Job." He scrutinizes me with an expression that conveys simultaneously both interest and a kind of suspended judgment.

I lean my elbows on the table and put my chin in my clenched fists. "Look," I say. "I'm a child of philosophical disenchantment. For me and my generation, carving up instrumental reason is the constitutive activity of the educated mind. But for all the years I've reported on this activity – indeed taken part in it – I've conceived of it as the sad business of postmodern thought. Now I'm wondering if it wasn't precisely your business; if you went to the trouble of opening up that old story – of interrupting the established ceremony of its retelling with what can only be called a philosophical argument – in order to make the point that suffering and reason are inseparable, that the former is the truth of the latter?"

He is silent for what seems like seven days. In reality, perhaps twenty seconds: just long enough for the tenuous confidence of middle age to drain away – long enough for me to superimpose the substance of my daydream on the afternoon, so distant as to seem itself now a product of imagination, when, confronting Henry Bugbee in the flesh, I was humbled by the austerity of genuine thought.

At last, he responds: "I'm not sure how to answer you. It's not that your question is irrelevant. But something in it worries me – a kind of presumption that everything is self-sufficient, discreet ... finished or settled. In my experience, the poet never takes that view. He never goes story-shopping on a whim, as if the materials of his craft had been harvested and sent to market somewhere. Absolutely not ..."

He's suddenly more animated. "I want to say instead that they somehow find *him* – that they show up on his doorstep one day wailing, foundlings, miraculous little eddies of memory in the tide of oblivion that forbids us access to the world our parents grew up in, let alone to earlier times. To make poetry is to shelter these foundlings, to celebrate their survival and help them flourish. Poets don't open up or interrupt finished stories – they protect and develop their organic possibilities. In this regard, no 'addition' they make to a pre-existing tale – whether by argument, dialogue, or criticism – should be arbitrary, merely clever, or in any way external."

There is a pause. "Do you know what I mean?" He's not being rhetorical. He wants me to understand.

"Tell me," I say.

"I mean that there's something more dignified and generous in poetry than autopsy and dissection," he says, "no matter how useful such things may seem from time to time. A poet makes himself responsible for the living reality of his narratives. And everything in poetry ought to bear witness to *that* responsibility!" Everything? I review now in a slight panic the long list of items on my original agenda. I stare hard at the table between us. While our author has been speaking, my hands have unclenched under my chin, migrated north, and quietly folded themselves over my mouth.

PATIENCE AND ENDURANCE

Among the benefits that accrue from imagining a conversation with the author of the Book of Job, none surpasses the possibility of being reminded somehow that the writer's first responsibility – like the actor and the reader! – is to bring a story to life. The business of writing – working out the structure of scenes and arguments, finding a tone or voice appropriate to the development of the matter in question, making your work at least minimally responsive to the larger intellectual and/or artistic contexts that provoke it, so often tempts you to forget this. Your workspace, after all, is the field of existential entanglements I evoked first in connection with Job's statements at 1:21, 2:10, and 3:3, and subsequently in following the contour of the argument his friends elaborate between Chapters 4 and 25. So masterful is our author's portrait of these entanglements, of these linguistic facades, especially in the context of post-Enlightenment philosophy, that we might easily take them for the substance of the work. But however much you learn about the dissection of instrumental reason from reading the Book of Job, there's something grander at stake. And it rises into view at least provisionally in the set of interventions given to our protagonist. Job's speeches surpass those of Eliphaz, Bildad, and Zophar, both superficially and profoundly. Superficially: in the sense that they elaborate a more coherent theology. Profoundly: in the sense that Job's multi-layered discourse embodies the irony I tagged at the beginning of the last chapter as the work of the text as a whole – and so the key to understanding the existential movement represented in its description of suffering. What might we grasp in advance as the frame of that movement?

On this, the tradition is univocal: in both word and deed, what our protagonist represents to us is *patience*. Indeed, we say proverbially of anyone displaying this virtue to an extraordinary degree that they have "the patience of Job." The origin of the locution is interesting. It is coined in a passage from the Epistle of James in the New Testament. There, the author of the letter counsels what the Revised Standard Version calls "steadfastness" in the face of suffering:

> You also be patient [*macrothumesate*]. Establish your hearts, for the coming of the Lord is at hand. Do not grumble, brethren, against one another, that you may not be judged; behold the Judge is standing at the doors. As an example of suffering and patience [*macrothumias*], brethren, take the prophets who spoke in the name of the Lord. Behold, we call those happy who were steadfast [*hypomeioantas*]. You have heard of the steadfastness of Job [*ten hypomone Iob*], and you have seen the purpose of the Lord, how the Lord is compassionate and merciful. (James 5:8–11)

Both *macrothumias* ("long-suffering") and *hypomone* ("remaining behind") may reasonably be translated as "patience." The Wycliffe Bible, for example, renders *ten hypomone Iob* as "the patience of Job" – in all likelihood the template for the King James rendering and the seed of the proverbial saying in English. But *hypomone* especially has other senses relevant to the phenomenon we want to track. It means also: the power to "to sustain blows" or simply "to endure." The second option is for me particularly interesting. It reinforces the idea of a defining *conatus* tested and attested to in suffering and, by extension, the ingredients of the "performative" integrity you rescued from Job's first three statements. *I* want to say: our protagonist is patient precisely in the sense that he *endures*. If this or something like it is true, the Epistle of James both reprises the limited sense we've made of what you might call the positive element of suffering and clarifies what's at stake in framing the set of Job's interventions. What you really want in articulating the nature of patience is an anatomy of endurance. And, in the phenomenological spirit appropriate to tracking descriptions as opposed to explanations, what you need to ask is: How does this anatomy present itself in the Book of Job?

Reviewing Job's speeches, I'm struck by a challenge diametrically opposed to the challenge presented by the chapters dedicated to Eliphaz, Bildad, and Zophar. What you must gauge in their interventions is the significance of an argument the character and fate of which are, in a certain sense, determined by repetition. Job himself, on the other hand, is mysteriously – sometimes maddeningly – Protean. His words are addressed alternately to his immediate interlocutors, to posterity, to the earth or life, and/ or to God. He speaks alternately as victim, judge, lawyer, theologian, ethicist, believer, and supplicant. The discourses themselves arrive wrapped alternately in anguish, in bitterness, in reasoned argument, in pious humility, and in prayer. Finally, and perhaps most vexingly, he appears alternately enduring and spiritually exhausted. (On at least two occasions Job seems to repudiate the virtue we want to understand in him. Cross-examining Eliphaz at 6:11, he asks: "What is my strength that I should wait? And what is my end, that I should be patient?" Responding to Zophar at 21:4: "As for me, is my complaint against man? Why should I not be impatient?") An arrangement of these rhetorical components that might reasonably be recognized as constituting steadfastness – let alone modelling it explicitly – is not obvious. Superficially at least, the sum of Job's interventions replicate on a grander scale the problem you've faced already in connection with the first three: you must rescue from diversity, from contradiction, some kind of telling integrity.

I was searching for an image in terms of which you might accommodate this problem when, on one of those mysterious paths of association that run through reflection, I found myself thinking about the old maps of the world you would have seen in elementary-school classrooms of the 1950s and 1960s. Their designers, wanting to discourage the illusion of an absolute east and west, used to extend the frame in both directions – to the point at which certain countries (India, Australia, parts of Russia) would appear at both the right and the left. As a seven-year-old, I found this distortion fascinating (Australia seemed to me far more interesting than North America, precisely because of its double). But the lesson was also clear enough – an announcement in two dimensions of the necessity to think in three. It strikes me now that you might imagine the speeches of Job spread out between Chapters 3 and 31 in the same spirit, namely, as if their linear arrangement were a necessary distortion, as if their Protean shape-shifting were itself an imperative to think "globally." It strikes me – to express it as I did in discussion of the comforters' chapters – that you might penetrate Job's interventions, not this time to follow or perform an autopsy of reason but to discover behind or beneath it the forces that give it life. At any rate, I want to suggest that if you plot our protagonist's speeches not simply in the two dimensions (before and after) of the theological dispute but in the space of the dramatic irony we've been exploring, you will uncover the anatomy of endurance. Specifically: it seems to me that in our poet's phenomenology of patience, something like pious humility – faith – is round the back of reason, and something like prayer – the primordial address of God – round the back of faith. How so exactly?

FROM REASON TO BITTERNESS

Begin with reason, the motor of the dialogue. Most evidently, Job's speeches respond to the arguments of Eliphaz, Bildad, and

Zophar. In the preceding chapter, I suggested to you that we might express what is crucial to those arguments – a theological position and its consequences for our protagonist – in the form of a syllogism:

MAJOR PREMISE: In God's world, reward follows virtue, punishment/suffering follows vice.
MINOR PREMISE: Job and his household are at present being punished/suffering.
CONCLUSION: Therefore, Job and his household must have been guilty of vice.

Job takes issue with every component of this inference. Its major premise, at least as presented by the comforters, implies an indefensible limit of divine power. If Eliphaz, Bildad, and Zophar are right, God's interventions in the world are themselves governed by – that is, subject to – the logic of reward and punishment. But God, in Job's view, is not subject to anything – least of all the kind of instrumental reason human beings use in accounting for their own status. On the contrary, by his power the *cosmos* itself is framed. Job stresses this omnipotence on several occasions, the first of which we find in the opening verses of Chapter 9:

But how can a man be just before God? If one wished to contend with him, one could not answer him once in a thousand times. He is wise in heart, and mighty in strength – who has hardened himself against him and succeeded? – he who removes mountains, and they know it not, when he overturns them in his anger; who shakes the earth out of its place, and its pillars tremble; who commands the sun, and it does not rise; who seals up the stars; who alone stretched out the heavens, and trampled the waves of the sea; who made the Bear and Orion, the Pleiades and the chambers of the south; who does great things beyond understanding, and marvelous things without number. (9:2–10)

The beginning of this speech appears to echo the voice in Eliphaz's vision ("Can mortal man be righteous before God," 4:17). Job's point, however, is different. It's not that human nature, or indeed his own nature as an individual, is necessarily corrupt; it's that no human integrity – including his own – can hope to withstand, ultimately, the assault of the infinite power that shapes the stars. Any doubt about this evaporates on examining the second part of Chapter 9. There, Job represents his own integrity precisely as that of an innocent *sustaining the blows* of such an assault:

> Though I am innocent, I cannot answer him; I must appeal for mercy to my accuser. If I summoned him and he answered me, I would believe that he was listening to my voice. For he crushes me with a tempest, and multiplies my wounds without cause; he will not let me get my breath, but fills me with bitterness. If it is a contest of strength, behold him! If it is a matter of justice, who can summon him? Though I am innocent, my own mouth would condemn me; though I am blameless, he would prove me perverse. I am blameless; I regard not myself; I loathe my life. It is all one, therefore, I say, he destroys both the blameless and the wicked. When disaster brings sudden death, he mocks at the calamity of the innocent. The earth is given into the hand of the wicked; he covers the faces of its judges – if it is not he, who then is it? (9:15–24)

The error of the comforters' major premise consists, then, in the presumption that the exercise of God's power is bounded by and therefore comprehensible in terms of moral reason. It is, in fact, utterly unbounded, humanly incomprehensible, and to all appearances indifferent to the behaviour of those who suffer its "disasters" and "calamities." But – if God's power is not bounded by moral reason, then suffering need not reduce to punishment. And if suffering need not reduce to punishment, the minor premise and the conclusion of the comforters' argument are also untenable; the fact of suffering need not be read as they read it. In sum: Job's radicalization of divine power – his insistence on what you might call the theologically sublime – effectively re-establishes the possibility of his own innocence.

Here we return, in the play of the dialogue itself, to the inscrutability of suffering remarked on by my old friend. "It is all one," for the innocent as for the guilty, for the "blameless" as for the "wicked." The "tempest" that crushes Job, that "multiplies [his] wounds *without cause*" (italics mine), arrives out of the blue. He simply finds himself put to the test. Among other things, this means in a very real sense that Job's philosophical response to Eliphaz, Bildad, and Zophar amounts to insisting on a phenomenology, as opposed to a deduction from abstract principles, on a resolute description of suffering, as opposed to an apology or explanation. His advocacy of the theologically sublime carries us back to the transition we tagged at 2:11–13 as the dialogue's centre of gravity; that is, to the evident mystery acknowledged and accommodated in shared silence. I want to draw your attention to two aspects of this advocacy that are relevant to sharpening our sense of what's at stake there.

Note first that the counterarguments of Chapter 9 are repeated and developed in the crowning phases of Job's discourse. Chapter 28, anticipating the great first chorus of Sophocles' *Antigone*,[4] opens with a hymn to the earth-transforming power of human ingenuity. At 28:9–11, for example, Job says: "Man puts his hand to the flinty rock, and overturns mountains by the roots. He cuts out channels in the rocks, and his eye sees every precious thing. He binds up the streams so that they do not trickle, and the thing that is hid he brings forth to light." But, as in *Antigone*, the hymn culminates in arrival at the limit of the thing praised. This happens abruptly at 28:12 – where you face the questions with which we began: "But where shall wisdom be found? And where is the place of understanding?"

There follows then a kind of portrait of the theologically sublime in negative space, where Job's point is that the terminus of wisdom and understanding lies beyond both the things of the world and the capacities of mind that know them:

Man does not know the way to it, and it is not found in the land of the living. The deep says, "It is not in me," and the sea says, "It is not with me." It cannot be gotten for gold, and

silver cannot be weighed as its price. It cannot be valued in
the gold of Ophir, in precious onyx or sapphire. Gold and
glass cannot equal it, nor can it be exchanged for jewels or
fine gold. No mention shall be made of coral or of crystal; the
price of wisdom is above pearls. The Topaz of Ethiopia cannot
compare with it, nor can it be valued in pure gold. Whence
then comes wisdom, and where is the place of understanding?
It is hid from the eyes of all the living, and concealed from the
birds of the air. Abaddon and Death say, "We have heard a
rumour of it with our ears." (28: 13–22)

If the origin of wisdom is "hid from the eyes of all the living," it
is, in fact, an act of hubris, of impiety, to rationalize the *cosmos*.
Our world operates in accordance with a power acknowledged
honestly and truly by human beings only in awe. Hence the divine
council reported famously and very bluntly at 28:28: "Behold the
fear of the Lord, *that* is wisdom."

Far from discouraging the cultivation of personal integrity
(on the mistaken assumption that such integrity must consist in
the application of moral reason), the wisdom attained in "the fear
of the Lord" imposes on you the imperative of resisting hubris,
of refusing the feigning imitation of divinity your own ingenuity
tacitly invites. It imposes on you, in other words, the explicit
responsibility of avoiding the sins of transgression. That is why
28:28 concludes "to depart from evil is understanding," and
why, in the final elaboration of his own code of behaviour in
Chapter 31, Job stresses honesty (31:5–6), fidelity (31:9–12),
respect (31:13–23), indifference to wealth (31:24–8), and mercy
(31:29–31). The antithesis in each case represents a pretense
of divinity. As a mode of concealment, deceit looks like sublimity.
As the expression of a certain liberty, infidelity looks like self-
determination. As an exercise of power, neglect or abuse of servants or of the poor looks like lordship. As the currency of human
economies, money and possessions look like the constituent elements of abundance. As a response to hatred, revenge looks like
warranted judgment. "The fear of the Lord," that is, acknowledgment of the sublimity of divine power, is embodied in the moral

integrity on which Job continues to insist, in spite of his wife's exhortation to abandon it (to "curse God and die"), in spite of the cold comfort/rage of his friends, in spite of the apparent counter-evidence of his own fortunes. "In spite of" these things, I say: but in this case the exceptions prove the rule. A God incapable of destroying even those who abide in proper awe of his power is not in the end omnipotent. The multiplication of Job's "wounds ... *without cause*" is a fate sanctioned by his own theological reasoning.

Note, secondly, the difference between Job's argument and the original gesture of comfort Eliphaz offers at 4:7–11 as response to the loss of refuge essential to suffering. For Eliphaz, comfort amounts to restoring the accommodation of the universal. The price of this restoration, as it turns out, is the other repository of sense: personal history. Accepting the theology of reward and punishment requires of Job the surrender of his self-understanding, of what he calls his "integrity." From Job's perspective, on the other hand, everything needs to be reversed. For him, comfort amounts to restoring the accommodation of personal history, of cleaving to the conviction that he has followed the code of behaviour elaborated in Chapter 31. The price of this self-assurance is the universal – the rationalization of fortunes in terms of reward and punishment. Job can persevere in the declaration of his innocence only as long as the divine "tempest" that "crushes" him remains inscrutable, morally incomprehensible. Eventually, we ought to produce an account of this odd symmetry, of the fact that our attempts to explain suffering (at least the suffering of the innocent) seem to require us to sacrifice one of our everyday accommodations in order to recover the other. But such an account is best provided after having framed reasoning/argument explicitly in the context of the dramatic irony by virtue of which our author elaborates his description of suffering, a project that requires, at a minimum, acquaintance with all the characters (God, Satan, Job, Eliphaz, Bildad, Zophar, Elihu) of our play. Here, I want to draw attention to what you might call the affective consequences of the arguments made by Job and his friends, for they seem to me essential in compassing both the real difference between them and what I called above the anatomy of endurance.

The affective consequence of the friends' argument, as I suggested in the previous chapter, is rage. So threatened are Eliphaz, Bildad, and Zophar by the resistance Job presents to the theology of reward and punishment in the course of stating his own case that they attack his very status as a rational agent (8:2, 11:2, 15:2, and 18:2, cf. pages 51 and 52 above). The trigger of this discursive violence is clear enough. Ideologues simply cannot afford to recognize recalcitrant cases. Exceptions to the rule are unforgivably subversive – ultimately intolerable. In contrast, the affective consequence of Job's argument is what he himself calls "bitterness." At 9:17–18, already cited above, for example, the sequence is clear: "For he crushes me with a tempest, and multiplies my wounds without cause; he will not let me get my breath, but fills me with bitterness."

The connection is reiterated at the beginning of Chapter 10: "I loathe my life; I will give free utterance to my complaint; I will speak in the bitterness of my soul."

Finally, in the opening verses of Chapter 27 come the first notes of the dialogue's proverbial coda, in the course of which Job will ask and answer the questions concerning wisdom and understanding (Chapter 28), articulate the foundations of his own the code of behaviour (Chapter 31) and – in the end – drive his friends back to the silence from which they emerge at 4:2:

> And Job again took up his discourse, and said: As God lives, who has taken away my right, and the Almighty, who has made my soul bitter; as long as my breath is in me, and the spirit of God is in my nostrils, my lips will not speak falsehood, and my tongue will not utter deceit. (27:1–4)

Job's bitterness is the opposite of his friends' rage in at least three important respects. First, while the trigger of the former is Job's claim to personal integrity, the trigger of the latter is the kind of moral universality espoused by Eliphaz at 4:7–11. Secondly, while what is enraging in Job's personal integrity is its irritating presence, its persistence in the face of the theology of reward and punishment, what embitters him in relation to moral universality, is its absence, that is, the inscrutability of divine power. Thirdly, while the friends rage in the face of the discord of the universal and the personal, Job laments the concord of his own suffering and the theologically sublime. On behalf of all the innocent sufferers who will succeed him, he pines for an explanation that cannot be given. At the end of the previous chapter, I suggested that the rage in which the friends' comfort culminates undoes the consolation of reason; that by its means Job is actively denied the refuge of universality. But even where that denial is exposed as unnecessary, as gratuitously cruel, where the sufferer has the gumption to insist on the accommodation of his personal integrity, reason takes its toll. Job's victory over the rage of his friends comes at the price of his own bitter nostalgia for moral universality.

FAITH AND PRAYER

All this would be incurably sad – and subject, ultimately, to the nihilism with which the dialogue opens at 3:3 – if it were the final word on the anatomy of endurance. But our author knows that the flatness of reason distorts Job's existential state in more or less the way old school maps distort the geography of the globe. He knows, in other words, that while pining for an explanation may be part of our protagonist's "integrity" – and so part of the phenomenology of his suffering – it is not the whole. That is why he makes a point of taking you behind the grinding tension of Job's bitterness, the affective consequence of his theology of the sublime, to another space, one capable of accommodating the stable essence of patience that arguments can represent only dynamically. Your best look at this space comes in the passage from Chapter 19 immortalized in the soprano aria that opens the third part of Handel's *Messiah*:

Oh that my words were written! Oh that they were inscribed in a book! Oh that with an iron pen and lead they were graven in the rock forever! For I know that my Redeemer lives, and at last he will stand upon the earth; and after my skin has been thus destroyed, then without my flesh I shall see God, whom I shall see on my side, and my eyes shall behold, and not another. (19:23–7)

The fervent plea of the first three sentences here assures you that the conviction expressed in the fourth will stand still, in spite of the "tempest" of 9:17 and in apparent contradiction of the extended cry of anguish in Chapter 3, which begins in despair ("Let the day perish wherein I was born") and ends with what looks for all the world like the involuntary forfeit of stillness ("I am not at ease, nor am I quiet; I have no rest; but trouble comes"). How are you to understand this dramatic turn?

In terms, it seems to me, of something like the existential psychology Kierkegaard elaborates in *Fear and Trembling* when reading the story of Abraham's near-sacrifice of Isaac (Genesis 22:1–19). The argument of that powerful little book is that neither the patriarch's actions nor his spiritual state can be accounted for adequately in a realm where moral reason is the highest court of appeal. Paradoxically, the story's impact depends on recognition of what Kierkegaard calls a "teleological suspension of the ethical,"[5] that is, a circumvention of duty in the service of a higher purpose. I say "paradoxically" because the circumvention in question does not and cannot culminate in the annulment of Abraham's moral "integrity." If it did, his actions would be psychologically indistinguishable from those of a murderer. Rather, Kierkegaard argues, the tension of the narrative resides in the fact that Abraham's ethical obligation to Isaac is simultaneously superseded *and* upheld. His being "put to the test" is a test precisely because he continues to love his son and cherish the possibility of his earthly happiness. Granting this, however, the ground of Abraham's action in the terrible moment when, at God's command, he raises the knife, must be positively unreasonable – a thoroughly irrational mix of resignation and hope. Kierkegaard writes simply: "[He has] resigned everything absolutely and then again seized hold of it all on the strength of the absurd."[6] Weighing this formula for my purposes, three points press.

First, set against the backdrop of 9:17 ("for he crushes me with a tempest, and multiplies my wounds without cause"), 3:26 ("I have no rest, but trouble comes") and related expressions of complaint, it represents almost perfectly the force of the declaration at 19:25–7 ("I know that my redeemer lives ... without my flesh I shall see God"). Insisting on the theologically sublime, on the unlimited power of God that "destroys both the blameless and the wicked," Job has, in effect, given up on rationality, on the power of explanation, on the stipulation of a universal law governing human action. At the same time, he wants to claim that his innocence will be acknowledged, that he will be redeemed, that the mystery he cannot fathom will be revealed to him.

Secondly, it reframes the estrangement of the universal and the personal that embitters Job qua rational agent in relation to what Kierkegaard calls "the absurd." The suggestion here, as indeed throughout *Fear and Trembling*, is that religious experience makes manifest a ground of human action greater, more challenging, and more profound than anything given to us by argument, and that Abraham's greatness stems from his apprehension of that ground.

Finally, and most importantly, this supra-rational apprehension is precisely what Kierkegaard calls "faith." The latter, rightly understood, is the still image of the restless bitterness to which the sufferer is driven by reason. And grasping it, you see that even bitterness itself can arise out of despair, stabilize it, and remake it as argument, only because what endures in it is faith.

It goes without saying that the profession of faith at 19:23–7 bears no resemblance to the kind of thing regularly pilloried in the past decade or so by evangelists of the new atheism.[7] There, on the "scientistic" side at least, the idea is that what is at stake in the quarrel of science and religion is an explanation of facts. Conversely, the dialogue between Job and his friends calls the power of rational explanation and account themselves explicitly into question. But – and here you touch the very foundation of our author's concept of patience or endurance – there is a sense in which Job's faith is more radical even than its Kierkegaardian twin. *Fear and Trembling* aims to rescue faith from the dynamo of German Idealism. Against the idea of a religion "within the limits of reason alone"[8] it presents "the absurd" as an absolute origin. The marvel of faith, on Kierkegaard's account, is its groundlessness. But on the side of the absurd facing away from reason – round back of what reason sees, to stay with our metaphor – there is another relation to the word, another dimension of language, that holds it in place. And here, as with the affective consequences of the dialogue, it shows itself to us in the difference between Job and his friends. Eliphaz, Bildad, and Zophar speak always and only *about* God; Job also speaks *to* him. An exhaustive compendium of these addresses isn't necessary for the purposes of the present argument. But a sample will support the point I want to make. At 7:17, you find the following:

> What is man that thou dost make so much of him, and that thou dost set thy mind upon him, dost visit him every morning, and test him every moment? How long wilt thou not look away from me, nor let me alone till I swallow my spittle?
> If I sin, what do I do for thee, thou watcher of men? Why hast thou made me thy mark? Why have I become a burden to thee? Why dost thou not pardon my transgression and take away my iniquity? For now I shall lie in the earth; thou wilt seek me, but I shall not be.

At 9:28:

> I become afraid of all my suffering, for I know thou wilt not hold me innocent. I shall be condemned; why then do I labour in vain? If I wash myself with snow, and cleanse my hands with lye, yet thou wilt plunge me into a pit, and my own clothes will abhor me.

At 13:20:

> Only grant two things to me, then I will not hide myself from thy face: withdraw thy hand far from me, and let not dread of

thee terrify me. Then call, and I will answer; or let me speak, and do thou reply to me.

At the outset of Chapter 14, drawing the first cycle of the dialogue to a close:

Man that is born of a woman is of few days, and full of trouble. He comes forth like a flower, and withers; he flees like a shadow, and continues not. And dost thou open thy eyes upon such a one and bring him into judgment with thee? Who can bring a clean thing out of an unclean? There is not one. Since his days are determined, and the number of his months is with thee, and thou hast appointed his bounds that he cannot pass, look away from him and desist, that he may enjoy, like a hireling, his day.

At 40:2–4, after the first of God's sermons from the whirlwind:

Behold, I am of small account; what shall I answer thee? I lay my hand on my mouth. I have spoken once, and I will not answer; twice, but I will proceed no further.

Finally, at 42:2–6, the last words our author puts in the mouth of his protagonist:

I know that thou canst do all things, and that no purpose of thine can be thwarted. "Who is this that hides counsel without knowledge?" Therefore I have uttered what I did not understand, things too wonderful for me which I did not know. "Hear and I will speak; I will question you, and you declare to me." I had heard of thee by the hearing of the ear, but now my eye sees thee; therefore I despise myself, and repent in dust and ashes.

I said above that, in the course of the theological argument, Job's behaviour as an interlocutor is exceedingly Protean. This is evident even if we limit our concern to tropes of divine address. Sometimes Job makes a ceremony of turning away from his friends in order to speak directly to God. Sometimes he merely promises to do so or imagines himself doing so, a step removed that warrants consideration in its own right. What bears notice here is only this: by the time we get to the epilogue (42:10–17), after the sermons from the whirlwind and Job's awestruck responses, it is clear that our protagonist's defining capacity, the power in suffering that sets him apart from his friends, that makes him who he is in the end, is unmediated communication with God, what in solitude and established rite you would ordinarily call prayer.

I take this to mean that for our author there is an essential connection between patience and divine address. The key to Job's endurance, its backbone (to return to the anatomical analogy with which we began), is a living conversation with God. Or again, in the phenomenology of suffering, what shows itself, ultimately, is the divine word. This is true in at least two senses. On the one hand, the narrative arc of the story, its linear progression, leads us from endurance to epiphany. The dramatic climax of Job's suffering is a kind of revelation. But beyond that and in supplement to it, as I've tried to indicate in this chapter, our author elaborates in the person of Job a non-linear relation of discourses, awareness of which invites you to apprehend in his every word the philosophical architecture of the space we first intuit distending out of his original cry of despair at 3:3. Behind that nihilism, as the dialogue reveals, is the shivering constancy of bitterness; behind that bitterness the still image of the Kierkegaardian absurd, of faith; behind that absurdity – affirming its truth not by argument but by living presence – the talk with God.

In the end, Job is separated from his friends by a second paradox, a puzzle diametrically opposed to the one we discovered by retracing the logic of the theology of reward and punishment. For Eliphaz, Bildad, and Zophar, the attempt at comfort ends in a kind of disenfranchising rage. For Job, the bitterness of despair culminates in the accommodation of divine presence. One line of existential intensity spirals downwards, the other upwards – as in Job's first words.

5

God and Satan Wager:
A Dramatic Interlude

"*Panim* is used in Hebrew in the plural form: man has more than one face."[1]

"By the way," says the voice on the other end of the line, "you should come to the scene studies tonight." It's my friend George. I've called him to check on the details of a poetry reading he's organizing. Our conversation now reminds him of the other event.

"Why?" I ask. "Do they involve people I know?" For the better part of the last decade, we've worked with drama students on a series of summer musicals – he as writer and/or director, I as vocal coach, arranger, and/or band member. As a result, I sometimes feel obligated to follow our performers in other productions.

"Yes," he says in response to my question. "But Peter's actually taken up your idea."

"What idea?" I ask.

"Staging the prologue to the Book of Job." Then he tells me that the focus of his playwriting course this time round has been literary adaptation, that, fresh from a talk we had had months before, he added the Book of Job to a long list of projects presented to students as possibilities at the beginning of term. Tonight, in addition to the prologue, I might see scenes from the *Iliad*, from Jane Austen's *Pride and Prejudice*, and from Sylvia Plath's *The Bell Jar*.

"When's Peter's thing?" I ask cautiously (I've already budgeted a couple of hours after supper for something else, and can't imagine dragging myself back to the office on the heels of a full evening of audience support).

"He's first after the intermission," George replies. Then, anticipating the time-management angle: "Get there by 9:15; you should be fine."

"Is it good?" I ask. (My experience with student projects in the past has been, to put it diplomatically, a mixed bag.)

He laughs. "Come and see ..."

I work from 7 p.m. to 9 p.m. I'm tired. By the time I walk over to the drama department in the damp cold of late November, my appearance there has reduced itself to an act of duty. George was right about the timing. I arrive during the intermission. The foyer of our little black-box theatre is filled with students, professors, and an assortment of people from the community. The authors, directors, and players of the Homer and Austen scenes mingle with the audience, receiving their kudos, recounting technical adventures and minor epiphanies. I find the mood light and almost immediately restorative. One of the great blessings of the university is the indomitable energy of its students – always game for a show, for some curtain to rise! I am greeted by one of them, who hands me the program as I make my way to a seat.

The set is almost completely bare. Stage centre-left there is an old-fashioned piano stool. Behind it, in a rough semi-circle, three sets of four-foot by eight-foot wooden risers. The two on the outside face the stool, their upstage ends angled slightly toward the centre. The one on the inside, perhaps three feet from its neighbour stage left, faces the audience. All pieces are painted a dull black, like the floor and the walls of the theatre itself. I am immediately disappointed. In my own directorial daydream, unconstrained by time or budget, I had imagined a set that might revolve like the giant Lazy Susans you see on *Saturday Night Live* – a circular platform divided in half by a wall separating "heaven" and "earth." On this model, each revolution would constitute a performance of that "going round back" that seems to me the governing principle of the Book of Job's dramatic irony. In effect, my Lazy Susan would show the audience the act of reading. How was that going to happen on a piano stool? And what about the actors? God and Satan and Job? The doomed children, the exasperated wife, and the messengers of disaster? Were they going to come and go in the dark? Would I have to hear their footfalls and rustling costumes for five or ten seconds, in transit between time and eternity?

I glance at the program. At the top of each page, there is an image appropriate to one of the adaptations (a kind of miniposter). Below these, in each case, there follows the list of credits. The image fronting Peter's *Job: The Prologue* is one of William Blake's engravings. Its composition is striking in terms of the dynamic I've tried to sketch in the last two chapters. On the left, you see a very old, miserable-looking Job kneeling on the ground; on the right, Eliphaz, Bildad, and Zophar, erect and full of resolve, pointing at our protagonist their fingers of accusation. The middle of the picture – the natural focal point – Blake leaves deliberately empty, as if he too wanted to make thematic the distance between their aspiration to comfort and its moralistic reality.

The lights go down. In the darkness there is a moment of silence. Then, almost imperceptibly at first, something that sounds like the crowd noise of a cocktail party. As the mingling of voices becomes more present, the light returns in a soft leafy pattern on the stage floor. A very warm spot then reveals a large figure, white dress shirt, pants, and shoes, sitting on the piano stool, facing stage right. I recognize the profile immediately. It's J.B., a veteran of two summer plays. His own hair and beard are full of white powder. Although he sits stock still, his facial expression conveys something vaguely like restless irritation. "The Lord God," I surmise, anticipating his role. No sooner have I registered this thought, than a second spot – colder, admixed with shades of blue and green – appears on the riser stage right. It illuminates a smaller figure, clad in denim from head to toe and sporting what appears to be the kind of half-mask made famous by the title character in Andrew Lloyd Webber's *Phantom of the Opera*. He faces the figure on the stool. "A Satan come of age in the eighties," I think. "This explains a lot ..."

The crowd cue fades. In a booming voice, J.B. intones the words: "Whence have you come?" (1:7).

His colleague (an actor I don't know) replies in a smaller, less-Biblical voice: "From going to and fro on the earth, and from walking up and down on it" (1:7).

As the line is spoken, J.B. makes a show of weighing it. Oddly un-God-like, I think. But it occurs to me, then, in his defence, that the dialogues of the Hebrew Scriptures might be impossible to deliver naturalistically, that the near-comedic melodrama of a movie like *The Ten Commandments* is as much a function of the resistances of source material as of overwrought Hollywood acting. J.B. continues:

"Have you considered my servant Job, that there is none like him on the earth, a blameless and upright man, who fears God and turns away from evil?" (1:8).

His question provokes the first in a series of surprises. The blue-green spot illuminating the original "Satan" snaps off, leaving the riser stage right in darkness. At virtually the same moment, it reappears on the upstage riser revealing a second "Satan," costume and mask identical to the first.

This actor, evidently a woman, faces stage left and speaks immediately: "Does Job fear God for nought? Hast thou not put a hedge around him and his house and all that he has, on every side? Thou hast blessed the work of his hands, and his possessions have increased in the land" (1:9–10).

At the words "in the land," the effect is repeated. The blue-green spot illuminating the second "Satan" snaps off, reappearing on the riser stage right. A third "Satan" – the set builder, as it turns out, of a show I worked on three years ago – faces stage left and, overlapping and interrupting his neighbour, completes the thought: "But put forth thy hand now, and touch all that he has, and he will curse thee to thy face" (1:11).

I wonder what I am to make of this. The actors speak in sequence, but the visual presentation suggests a chorus – or at least a transgression of individual consciousness. I note that, although J.B. acknowledges the second and third "Satans" with a slight movement of his head, he does not turn to face them. The effect is dreamlike, almost hallucinogenic, as if the Biblical scene was really just a figment of his imagination. As I ponder the theological consequences of that possibility, I'm recalled to the action by J.B.'s response: "Behold, all that he has is in your power; only upon himself do not put forth your hand" (1:12).

The actors freeze. On a slow fade the stage grows dark. As the lights go down, a sound cue comes up: the distant cries of people in distress, morphing slowly into the howling of a violent windstorm. The transition takes maybe ten seconds. The cyclone continues in the dark for another five to ten. Then light and sound reverse. The windstorm dies away as the set becomes visible again. I see the same four figures. Now, though, J.B. faces stage left like the others. He is dressed in black from head to toe. His hair and beard, I notice, have resumed their natural colour. This I find intriguing. The noise and the darkness of the scene change might have accommodated his costume change, especially if he was wearing the black clothes under the whites. But I can't fathom the quick change of makeup. It would surely take a good three minutes over the sink to wash yourself that clean.

The Satans around J.B. remain motionless long enough to establish the tableau for the audience. The former "set builder" then reanimates theatrically and speaks: "The oxen were ploughing and the asses feeding beside them; and the Sabeans fell upon them and took them, and slew the servants with the edge of the sword; and I alone have escaped to tell you" (1:14–15).

The voice is metallic, recorded. The actor moves his mouth and his hands like someone lip-synching a song. It is thought-provoking. Peter's script retains only the direct speech of the characters. Here is a way of making Satan's agency – more obvious in the third-person narration of the Biblical text – evident. I find myself wondering suddenly about the status of Job's messengers. Melville took from them the motto for the epilogue of *Moby Dick*,[2] effectively pushing Ismael's finely detailed account of the human condition, of love and obsession, of epiphany and disaster, back into the words "and I alone have returned to tell you." Is the messenger before me – speaking out of Satan's body – somehow an epitome of narratives to come? J.B.'s face contorts, and I register consciously a second surprise: He is now Job! What does that mean? The female Satan upstage channels a second metallic voice, reporting the destructive fire from heaven and the murderous exploits of the Chaldeans. Her colleague stage right then finishes with "the unkindest cut of all," the death of Job's children in the storm. J.B. straightens his back on the piano stool, as if to marshal all the dignity that posture can possibly bear. Then, staring at a spot on the stage three feet in front of him, he says quietly – so quietly I find myself leaning forward to hear: "Naked I came from my mother's womb, and naked shall I return; the Lord gave, and the Lord has taken away; blessed be the name of the Lord" (1:21).

Change of scene: As the stage darkens, we hear a recorded echo of the word "Lord." It grows in volume and overlaps itself at shorter and shorter intervals, until the consonants at the beginning and end disappear and the "o" becomes a kind of wail. The single voice then fragments – sliding, overdubbed at different pitches. The point of greatest vocal chaos comes at full blackout and continues for three or four beats. After that, the cue effectively reverses itself. The disparate voices merge on a single pitch, as happens sometimes in the chanting exercises of a yoga class. The unison is refined and tranquilized. As it begins to grow remote and die away, the soft leafy light pattern of the first scene returns, uncovering the Lord God and his Satanic council precisely as we left them.

J.B.'s second quick change is every bit as impressive as the first. But I am distracted – or rather completely engaged – by the soundscape. Peter and/or his technical director will have had theatrical reasons for designing it as they did. But whatever they intended, the suggestion to the audience is that what *we* hear as wailing, as the lament of the sufferer, reaches God as song. Suddenly I find myself on the horns of a very uncomfortable dilemma. Either the song of heaven is a distortion – in which case God himself is deluded (a kind of proto-ideologue who can't tell the difference between beauty and horror) – or the chant he hears is the truth of a suffering which deludes *us* so completely that all our attempts to express what is at stake in it are doomed to fail. In the first case, it looks for all the world as if God's delusion would keep him from loving and/or restoring us; in the second, as if our delusion would make restoration utterly incomprehensible, as if Job's despair were really our final word on the human condition. Needless to say, I need to think this through.

Meanwhile, on the stage in front of me, our narrative continues in that oddly timeless "later on" of myths and folktales ("Again there was a day when the sons of God came to present themselves before the Lord, and Satan also came among them" [2:1]). J.B.'s Biblical script requires him to repeat his first line. It is addressed, as before, to the actor stage right: "Whence have you come?" (2:2).

It seems to me that he makes a point of intoning it as he did originally, in order to emphasize the epic style of the text. His colleague replies in the same spirit: "From going to and fro on the earth, and from walking up and down on it" (2:2).

There is a kind of temporal indeterminacy just below this text's surface to which the actual seeing and hearing of these repeated lines helps draw attention. I now wonder how much "human" time has elapsed between the first day in heaven and the second? A week? Three years? Has Job managed to reconcile himself to his initial misfortune? Has the moment at which he might have cursed God on this account come and gone? As I try to imagine the lived experience of the period that might have intervened "in the land of Uz" between the two celestial scenes, it occurs to me that the movement in stasis I described – first with respect to the despair that pours out of Job's stoicism at 1:21 and 2:10, then with respect to the rage that devolves from the friends' theology of reward and punishment in the cycles of the dialogue – offers at least the possibility of extended accommodation. The existential contradiction of suffering that our author makes so fluid, so perceptible, by pushing stoicism against its limit explicitly in Job's first three statements, could also play out at a far more glacial pace: one measured in generations, in eras, even in cultural traditions. How many characters, in literature, in politics, in families and communities of all kinds, live their entire lives in the slippage of their espoused convictions? In how many of those ages historians demarcate to help us make sense of our collective past do we find institutions and values surreptitiously in decline? And the post-Enlightenment European philosophy I try to rehearse in broad strokes for the Bugbee-faced author of my daydreamed interview? Isn't it, in relation to the entire twenty-five hundred years of intellectual and spiritual labour with which it takes issue, roughly what Job's cry at 3:3 ("Let the day perish wherein I was born") is to his interventions at 1:21 and 2:10 ("the Lord gave, and the Lord has taken away"; "Shall we receive good at the hand of the Lord, and shall we not receive evil?"): namely, the acknowledgment that any meaning that might once have animated our rational processes has now drained away? The temporal indeterminacy of the movement from Chapter 1 to Chapter 2, framed by the repetition of the original exchange between God and Satan, allows us to imagine Job's suffering not only as a contradiction governing episodes *in* life (episodes we might avoid with a run of dumb luck), but the deep structure of life itself.

There's a similarly thought-provoking psychological indeterminacy in Satan's remark alone. Indeed, it strikes me now, looking on from the audience, as intentionally opaque. Someone following the action but unacquainted with the source material would surely have expected a report on Job's dossier, an assessment of his performance when "put to the test." Has his tormentor already lost interest in his fate? Was there subsequently so much on his agenda that Job simply slipped his mind? Or – was he unexpectedly shamed and surpassed by his victim, so that he's now hoping to avoid discussion of a confident prediction that clearly came to nothing? Turning over this last possibility – the most dramatically appealing – I find myself picturing a freer adaptation of our story (Peter has stayed resolutely with the text of the Revised Standard Version of the Bible) in which God and Satan are characters in a *Pride and Prejudice*–like comedy of manners. Sparring with his rival, the Lord amuses himself and his courtiers by trying to coax an acknowledgment of failure from the pleasantries of their apparently innocent small-talk ("So good to see you, my friend! It's been far too long. Do tell us what's new in the world"). In such a scenario, Satan's confession need not take the form of a direct statement. Indeed it's better if it doesn't – that is, better if he demonstrates his shame by taking refuge in a generality that is awkwardly evasive, that makes a show of what it is concealing (God: "So ... what *have* you been up to?" Satan: "Um ... nothing really. I've been here and there").

J.B. is about to answer his interlocutor. Although he remains seated on the piano stool, he leans forward now with his hands on his knees, like a lawyer springing a well-laid trap in cross-examination: "Have you considered my servant Job, that there is none like him on the earth, a blameless and upright man, who fears God and turns away from evil? He still holds fast to his integrity although you moved me against him, to destroy him without cause" (2:3).

I notice that, while Satan's repeated line frames a difference between the first and second celestial scenes – what you hear initially as a straightforward report on his activities sounds subsequently like the suppression, or at least the forgetting, of a particular case – God's refrain conveys perfect consistency. What he says of Job in Chapter 1 stands. There's no ambiguity. The words mean exactly and only what they meant at the outset. At the same time, the new material from 2:3 ("He still holds fast to his integrity, although you moved me against him, to destroy him without cause") highlights what you might call a reversal of agency. In the first scene, God is called upon by Satan to let him test Job; in the second, Satan is called upon by God to admit that Job has passed the test. If the book of Job *were* a comedy of manners, Satan's position at this point would be intolerable. Explicit reference to the wager goes beyond putting him in the position of evading talk about a failure the courtly audience recognizes. God now calls him out in no uncertain terms. He cannot even pretend to save face.

Perhaps, for our author, etiquette of this kind applies even in the very serious situation he portrays at 2:2–6. It would go some measure of the way toward explaining the ferocity of Satan's response, now neither cagey nor Machiavellian but literally homicidal. As in the first scene, Peter splits the text between the actors upstage centre and stage left. Satan 2 virtually shouts: "Skin for skin! All that a man has he will give for his life" (2:4).

Her colleague, speaking at the same fevered pitch, finishes the thought: "But put forth thy hand now, and touch his bone and his flesh, and he will curse thee to thy face" (2:5).

At this point, my 9 p.m. fatigue has disappeared entirely. I find myself suddenly filled with gratitude for the little studio and the university that houses it. Once, on the opening night of a summer play a few years back, I remember George reminding those about to take this same stage of the actor's tremendous privilege. "You live in a world of imagination," he said then, "a world you help create and bring to life!" Just now, I feel like the direct beneficiary of that work. The imaginations of the students involved in this little study have stimulated my own in ways I couldn't have anticipated even an hour earlier. And although the event produces the usual unintentional hiccups of amateur theatre (near the end of the blackout between Scenes 1 and 2 someone upsets what turns out to be a table set for the Plath scene, so that, as the windstorm cue dies away, we hear knives and forks clattering on the floor, followed by very audible profanity), its overall effect is magical. Step by step, my own vague predispositions as to how the prologue might be dramatized are superseded by an actual performance.

In the context of that performance, we've arrived at the thing that interests me most: the moment God grants Satan licence to take from Job everything but his life. From the standpoint of theology, it seems to me the biggest moment in the entire story. It depicts the genuine origin of a suffering bounded only by the bare condition for its possibility (i.e., the sufferer's survival). My interest stems not from some pre-existent confidence about how you might present this origin to an audience. On the contrary, it fascinates me because my own readerly experience of it is utterly inscrutable. How will J.B. put it across? He straightens up on the piano stool, head turned slightly upward, still in profile. The posture appears meant to suggest that his response will be directed to the Satanic collective – or at least to no one of them in particular. His body is quiet, his face relaxed, almost slack. "Behold he is in your power," he says rather blankly, "only spare his life" (2:6).

I am unmoved. But that's no surprise. I wasn't expecting J.B. simply to lift the veil on a 2,500-year-old mystery. On the contrary, I wanted his real-time performance mostly to push against, so I could say to myself, "the line would work better if it were delivered faster or slower, more or less forcefully, after a beat or two of silence, while staring at a spot on the floor, as his 'Job' did at the end of the first day on earth," etc.

But as I now carry out this experiment, putting myself in his place, I find the line as impenetrable for the actor in me as for the reader. Would it have made more sense delivered in a spirit of resignation? The implication there would be that God is somehow bound to satisfy Satan, that he has no choice but to extend the wager. But there's not a shred of evidence in the theological traditions of the Hebrew Scriptures to support that view.

Would the line work better delivered in anger? The implication there would be that Job has done something to provoke God's ire – the inference, of course, developed by Eliphaz, Bildad, and Zophar. But God himself says explicitly (and for the second time) at 2:3 that Job is blameless and righteous and that "there is none like him on the earth."

What if God were ironic, here, like Socrates? As if he were saying to Satan, "by all means let's explore your hypothesis," but then *sotto voce*, "to the point where it collapses under the weight of its own contradiction." The implication here would be that Satan needs to be taught a lesson, like Thrasymachus, Callias, Meno, or one of the other young "upstarts" that populate Plato's dialogues. But it is one thing to put a rival's convictions to the test, to risk compromising his expert's reputation; quite another to ruin the life of a faithful servant in order prove your point to a third party. You forgive Socrates' mischief, because the intellectual discomfort it produces falls on those who deserve it. In relation to Job's suffering, on the other hand, the playfulness of such an irony would be inexcusably heartless.

Could representation of heartlessness itself be the object of the exchange? The implication here would be that God is, in human terms, a kind of sociopath, that he regards Job's suffering as the means to an end, and doesn't for a moment weigh its consequences in the balance. This comes close to the effect J.B. actually produces. But it makes nonsense both of the apparently compassionate restoration of Job's fortunes reported in the epilogue and of the book's subsequent reception/history.

Finally, what if, developing the flipside of that experiment, you were to insist on delivering the line "lovingly" (presuming you could find a way of communicating that with no help whatsoever from the words that comprise it), in a tone that would mirror deliberately the tender praise of Job at 2:3? That might produce, at least momentarily, an illusion of consistency for actor and audience. But it would also play the expression of the text explicitly against its content, leaving us, at a minimum, with the question of what "love" here could possibly mean.

The fact is – I find myself unable to improve on J.B. No delivery of the text at 2:6 I try on makes it possible to accommodate it sensibly in the scene, the wider context of the book, or the subsequent theological/philosophical tradition. The word of God here simply repels my options for performing it. I understand it syntactically – as a statement, as a directive – but I can't imagine what feeling it is supposed to convey. The line seems to me sentimentally impossible! It's not a question here of its discursive complexity. When Malvolio says, "for every reason excites to this, that my lady loves me," I have no problem intuiting both that he believes it and that it's false. When King Oedipus says, "I will start afresh; and bring everything to light," I have no problem grasping both his innocent resoluteness and the foreshadowing of his ruin. Comedies and tragedies call on us regularly to recognize in dialogue or soliloquy the play of two (or more) sentimental codes. The problem with 2:6 is that, to all appearances, it resists such coding completely. Mulling this over, I find words for a thought that has troubled me, half-baked and inchoate, since the beginning of my study: the word of God here illuminates a domain of our experience that lies beyond feeling and fellow-feeling. The first great lesson of his wager with Satan is the simple revelation of that domain. But if that's true, its analysis ought eventually to yield the concept of a love more existentially basic than fellow-feeling, a love – notwithstanding the catechisms and children's stories of the Judeo-Christian tradition – that is nothing like the sheltering embrace of your human father.

The lights have faded. In the grey-black, the players hold their positions – statues in silhouette. I hear something like the buzzing of insects, mingled with voices of lament – but at what seems like a far greater distance than in previous scene transitions. The cue has been established for six or seven seconds when, from the shadow figure on the middle riser, I hear the words: "Do you still hold fast your integrity? Curse God and die" (2:9).

J.B. replies: "You speak as one of the foolish women would speak. Shall we receive good at the hand of God, and shall we not receive evil?" (2:10).

There are three long beats of silence. His question lingers in the air. Then the lights (even in the house) come on all at once, like the power returning after an outage. I blink and there is a moment of uncertainty as to whether the show is over. But the Satans have now begun to move. They step together like dancers, always in profile, facing stage left, migrating to a spot at the audience right of J.B., just in front of the stage-left riser. For the stage-right Satan, this involves nothing much more than a kind of stylized walking; for his colleagues a more laboured choreography of movements sideways and backwards. At the end of their journey, they stand shoulder to shoulder, downstage to upstage, so that, if you're seated in front of them, as I am, the body of the nearest conceals almost entirely those of the other two.

Draw back a moment. I want to you to understand that what happens next – the finale of this little production, as it turns out – is actually the trigger of my reporting the entire event. That's because it seems to me to condense into a single gesture the way forward for our phenomenology of suffering. In effect, it *shows* you the truth of the movements I described first in terms of Job's interventions at 1:21, 2:10, and 3:3, then in terms of the devolution of the friends' theology of reward and punishment, and finally in terms of the anatomy of our protagonist's endurance. How so? For a moment J.B. and his courtiers freeze back to back. Then each begins to turn. J.B. pivots slowly off the piano stool, stage left. In one fluid motion (impressive for a man of his size), he is on his knees, open to the audience, although angled stage left. His arms drop to his sides in apparent exhaustion. By means of this movement, you learn the secret of his quick change. I should have guessed it earlier. On his left side he is made up as God – white powdered hair and beard – on the right as Job. His costume is white on the left, black on the right. These effects were concealed by the static, two-dimensional blocking of the short scenes. All he had to do in the intervening blackouts was rotate 180 degrees. At the same moment J.B. turns to face them, the Satans turn as well. Their half-masks now revolve upstage, and we see their human faces. Their costumes too are motleys – denim on the right, black cloth of some kind on the left. The one closest to me winds down into a sitting position, right leg tucked under his body, left drawn up so that his chest is almost resting on his knee. The woman leans out over him, facing right but angled downstage. The set builder remains standing, head drooping to one side, like someone at the end of a long-distance run. All six arms extend towards J.B., fingers pointing.

And suddenly I grasp the design. The actors' tableau reconstitutes the Blake engraving! Here though (in contrast to the program), it's not simply the still image of a legend. It's the terminus of a movement, of a choreography. And in that context, it captures more than the friends' accusation, more than Job's suffering endurance. It argues – in the powerful mode of *showing* you – that behind the theology of reward and punishment is Satan's rage! Behind Job's despair, God's wager!

The performance ends and the actors take a bow. In the foyer of the theatre afterward, I make a point of speaking to Peter. "Well … I loved it!" I say sincerely. "You know I've been trying to write a kind of commentary on the Book of Job on and off for a few years now. You really gave me some things to think about."

"Thanks for coming," he says modestly.

"I especially liked the homage to Blake at the end," I say, "the way it 'settles in' as everyone does an about-face."

"I kinda stole that idea from the Flying Karamazov Brothers,"[3] Peter laughs. "You know, from that version of *The Comedy of Errors* we pulled off YouTube – um, not last summer but the summer before. Remember? Dromeo runs on the spot one way, then spins in mid-air and turns out to be someone else running the other?"

"I do remember, now that you mention it," I say, "but here's my real question – and it's funny because it's exactly the kind of thing I'm trying to sort out in my own stuff: how come the Satans turn out to be the friends?"

"Honestly?" he asks, grinning broadly. I wait expectantly. "Well, for the same reason they play the messengers and Mrs Job … I only had four actors."

6

Elihu Takes Up the Argument

AFTER THE DIALOGUE

My night at the theatre happened to come in one of those periods
of uncertainty I see now as endemic to philosophical writing. I
had been thinking long and hard about our author's representa-.
tion of the experience of being "put to the test." My working
hypothesis, as I said earlier, was that he wanted to open up the
original tale (the proverbial "foundling" on his own doorstep), in
order to nurture the phenomenology of suffering latent in it.
Taking the existential reversals framed in Job's first interventions
as a kind of epitome, I saw him elaborating – as constitutive of
that suffering – two central ironies: the irony by means of which
our conventional discourses of comfort, founded on the instrumental reason of the theology of reward and punishment, fall
first into inflexible ideology, then into rage; and the irony by
means of which the discourses of bitterness, expressed first as
nihilistic despair, ascend through faith to the intimacy with God
characteristic of genuine patience. You discover the arc of the first
transition in the speeches of Eliphaz, Bildad, and Zophar; that of
the second in the speeches of Job himself.

　But development of this general hypothesis notwithstanding,
significant questions remained for me, both in relation to what I
had brought to the text as a reader and to what the text itself
presents and represents. I came to the Book of Job with the
intuition that it could help sort out the central issue that had

developed for me in the course of teaching Heidegger, Plato, and the philosophical tradition on the one hand, and Euripides, Kafka, and the literary tradition on the other: the existential play of love and indifference, of accommodation and abandonment. While this issue is undoubtedly central for our author, he steadfastly refuses to reconcile these conditions by making one of them subordinate to the other. On the contrary, the ironies of the dialogue show us, in effect, each of them disappearing into its putative opposite. The friends' comfort aims at restoration of the refuge of universality, at accommodating our protagonist's suffering in an account of the basic intelligibility of the world. But the price of this accommodation is abandonment of the integrity that constitutes him as a person. Conversely, Job's own bitterness is an expression of his perceived abandonment by God. But the intimacy of its expression – in the unshakeable conviction of his faith, in his direct address of God – attests a kind of accommodation not even death can shatter ("For I know that my redeemer lives, and at last he will stand upon the earth; and after my skin has been thus destroyed, then without my flesh I shall see God, whom I shall see on my side" – 19:25–7).

Our author's proposition appears to be that abandonment is round back of accommodation, accommodation round back of abandonment. The condition reflected in such a proposition, however, is still far from clear *phenomenologically* – by which I mean it has yet to show itself to us in the arc of the narrative. If my working hypothesis is to be consolidated – if I am to convince you that the Book of Job is best read as a careful description of how we find ourselves put to the test – I need to show how, following the play of experience itself, our author makes the revolutions in which Job seems simply immersed, explicit and comprehensible not only to the reader but to his protagonist.

If accounting for something like this self-discovery constitutes the philosophical aspiration of the Book of Job – if the story our author wants to tell is the story of how our protagonist comes, as it were, face to face with the ironies that frame his suffering, that frame life itself – then, by the process of elimination, if nothing else, we should expect to see the arrival of this elevated consciousness in the two scenes of the drama that follow the dialogue: Elihu's renewal of the friends' moral argument (Chapters 32–7) and God's awe-inspiring speeches from the whirlwind (Chapters 38–41). This, in turn, would allow us to conceive of the text as a phenomenology in two parts, book-ended and illuminated by the prologue (Chapters 1 and 2) and the epilogue (Chapter 42). In part one (Chapters 3 to 31), our author shows us the sufferer lost in the ironies that define him. In part two (Chapters 32 to 41), by means I must try now to eluci-date, he shows the sufferer finding himself backstage of these iro-nies. My questions, then, are the following: Do the arguments of Elihu and the whirlwind speeches lend themselves to such a read-ing? Is it possible to apprehend in them a coming to conscious-ness of the forces already at work in the speeches of Eliphaz, Bildad, and Zophar, of Job, and to grasp in that development the crowning phase of an account of experience itself?

THE PROBLEM OF ELIHU

On a first or second pass through the Book of Job, the character of Elihu seems particularly hard to manage. His very presence in the work is mysterious. We see him neither in the prologue (where the friends are introduced at 2:11) nor the epilogue (where God says to Eliphaz at 42:7, "My wrath is kindled against you and against your *two* friends," where the narrator reports the subse-quent pardon of "Eliphaz the Temanite and Bildad the Shuhite and Zophar the Na'amathite" following Job's prayer on their behalf at 42:9). Instead, he appears, ostensibly from nowhere, at the beginning of Chapter 32. In spite of the fact that he makes the same kinds of arguments that exercised our protagonist in previ-ous chapters, Job doesn't respond to him. His intervention is overtaken, instead, by the storm of God's word, in which the human voice effectively dies away. All of this conspires to make him a strangely spectral figure, unnoticed and unacknowledged. If you perform the experiment of excising his lines, of pasting God in immediately following Chapter 31, there is a sense in which the narrative as a whole is simpler and more consistent. This has led a number of scholars to entertain the idea that Elihu's arguments are interpolations of a later editor.[1]

On the other hand, some very influential readers have taken these arguments to be, in one way or another, indispensable. Both Gregory and Aquinas read the stinging rebuke with which the whirlwind speech famously opens – "Who is this that darkens my counsel by words without knowledge?" – as directed at Elihu, not Job.[2] At a minimum, that would make him structurally essential, the prod of the narrative's denouement, the instantiation of the human folly God rouses himself to correct. Calvin, in contrast, sees Elihu as "the organ of the Spirit of God," the presage of the epiphany that follows directly.[3] In this reading, his absence in the epilogue is evidence of his having avoided the errors of Eliphaz, Bildad, and Zophar, of having provided Job the model of speech God approves at 42:7. Most interesting for our purposes, Elie Wiesel draws attention to a Talmudic commentary that associates Elihu with Satan, that reads the mysterious appearance of a fourth "friend" as the covert return of an angel unlikely to have left the dispute so central to his wager with God in the hands of mediocre advocates.[4]

One significant advantage of taking Elihu's arguments as a moment of Job's self-discovery, that is, of his coming to consciousness of the forces at work in his suffering, is the potential of such a reading for reconciling these disparate positions (each of which strikes me as valid in some measure). It is possible, I think, in terms of this reading, to grasp Elihu as at once appropriately spectral *and* essential. How? Looking now explicitly at Chapters 32 to 37, consider, at least provisionally, the following questions: 1) What do Elihu's arguments have in common with those of Eliphaz, Bildad, and Zophar? 2) What is novel about them? 3) What sense can we make of Job's non-response to Elihu? 4) Is there a case for taking seriously the Talmudic suggestion that Elihu represents the return of Satan? 5) If so, how do we square that crucial role with the otherwise spectral nature of his presence in the narrative?

COLD COMFORT REVISITED

In response to question 1): come back first to the issue of silence. You'll recall its signal importance in the transition from prologue to dialogue (2:11–13). The wordless communion Job shares with his friends for "seven days and seven nights" constitutes both the gravitational centre of *his* apparently contradictory statements at 1:21, 2:10, and 3:3, and the high point of *their* attempt at comfort. As I suggested earlier, the breach of this fragile solidarity in our protagonist's eventual cry of despair ("Let the day perish wherein I was born") provokes the long argument. And although they do not say it outright, in both a generous and a self-serving sense, Eliphaz, Bildad, and Zophar want nothing so much as restoration of what they've lost – namely, Job's silence.

As the curtain rises on Elihu's scene in Chapter 32, he is scandalized, not by this prospect (for him too, restraining Job is an absolute necessity), but by its almost comic reversal in the hurly-burly of the foregoing quarrel – that is, by the *friends'* speechlessness: "They are discomfited, they answer no more; they have not a word to say. And shall I wait, because they do not speak, because they stand there, and answer no more?" (32:15–16). The question, of course, is rhetorical. Elihu's intervention will aim at restraining – at silencing – Job's apostasy, at putting a definitive end to his expressions of bitterness. It will aim, in other words, at redeeming what the friends have botched, at saving them from their own mediocrity. A final flourish invoking his discursive powers at the end of Chapter 33 makes the substance of this aspiration sun-clear:

> Give heed, O Job, listen to me; *be silent* and I will speak. If you have anything to say, answer me; speak, for I desire to justify you. If not, listen to me; *be silent*, and I will teach you wisdom. (33:31–3, italics mine)

If you then track through the speech that follows with a view to discerning the wisdom that Job's eventual silence is to welcome and accommodate, you find, among other things, an expression of the theology of reward and punishment that could have been pinched directly from Eliphaz and company. You are assured, for example, that the good prosper and the evil are punished. At 34:10–11, Elihu says:

Therefore, hear me, you men of understanding, far be it from God that he should do wickedness, and from the Almighty that he should do wrong. For according to the work of a man he will requite him, and according to his ways he will make it befall him.

And later in the same chapter (21–8) having hit the stride of his sermon:

For his eyes are upon the ways of a man, and he sees all his steps. There is no gloom or deep darkness where evildoers may hide themselves. For he has not appointed a time for any man to go before God in judgment. He shatters the mighty without investigation, and sets others in their place. Thus, knowing their works, he overturns them in the night, and they are crushed. He strikes them for their wickedness in the sight of men, because they turned aside from following him, and had no regard for any of his ways, so that they caused the cry of the poor to come to him, and he heard the cry of the afflicted.

Echoing Zophar (11:5–6) and Eliphaz (15:7–9), Elihu further assures you that the potential counter-evidence of Job's integrity – indeed, all potential counter-evidence – is a mirage of human perception:

Behold, in this you [Job] are not right. I will answer you. God is greater than man. Why do you contend against him, saying 'He will answer none of my words'? For God speaks in one way, and in two, though man does not perceive it. (33:12–14)

Finally, and as a direct consequence of this non-falsifiability, you are assured that any voice raised against the theology of reward and punishment must be irrational, vacuous:

> Surely God does not hear an empty cry, nor does the Almighty regard it. How much less when you say that you do not see him, that the case is before him, and you are waiting for him! And now, because his anger does not punish, and he does not greatly heed transgression, Job opens his mouth in empty talk, he multiplies words without knowledge. (35:13–16)

In short, all the essential moments of the friends' argument are recuperated in Elihu's intervention: the move to silence what appears to be impious nihilism, the endorsement of the theology of reward and punishment, the ideological prohibition of counter-evidence and the consequent rage at enduring dissent. On the one hand, then, Elihu reinforces the position of his older interlocutors by mirroring it.

ELIHU'S PROGRESS

But, in response to question 2): his argument is by no means limited to that kind of reflection. In at least two important respects, Elihu breaks new ground. You see it first in what you might call loosely his approach to time. For Eliphaz, Bildad, and Zophar, theological explanation is an exercise in making sense of the past. The suffering God sanctions is punishment for things done or left undone – whether by individuals (Zophar: "Know then that God exacts of you less than *your* guilt deserves" – 11:6, italics mine), by collectives (Bildad: "If your children have sinned against him, he has delivered them into the power of their transgression" – 8:4), or by human beings qua human (Eliphaz: "For affliction does not come from the dust, nor does trouble sprout from the ground, but man is born to trouble as the sparks fly upward" – 5:6–7). To understand the world, even as dominated by apparently undeserved suffering, is to grasp the significance of what has been. While Elihu accepts such assessments as a dimension of the explanation of suffering, he does not regard them as exhaustive. He sees, quite rightly, that your sense of the world depends as much on projecting a future as on recouping a past. For him, indeed, the meaning of suffering ought to be grasped, above all, in projective terms – as a prod to emergent self-understanding, to self-development, to perfection of the very integrity Job prizes. Look, for example, at the continuation of the argument, beginning with the passage at 33:12 cited above:

> Behold, in this you are not right. I will answer you. God is greater than man. Why do you contend against him, saying, "He will answer none of my words"? For God speaks in one way, and in two, though man does not perceive it. In a dream, in a vision of the night, when deep sleep falls upon men, while they slumber in their beds, then he may turn man aside from his deed, and cut off pride from man; he keeps back his soul from the Pit, his life from perishing by the sword. Man is also chastened with pain upon his bed, and with continual strife in his bone, so that his life loathes bread, and his appetite dainty food. His flesh is so wasted away that it cannot be seen; and his bones which were not seen stick out. His soul draws near the Pit, and his life to those who bring death ... Behold God does all these things, twice, three times, with a man, to bring back his soul from the Pit, that he may see the light of life.
> (33:12–22, 29–30)

Suffering on this account is a "chastening" that enlightens. (The passage anticipates the argument of Boethius's Lady Philosophy many centuries later. Weighing his good and bad fortune, she concludes simply: *illa fallit, haec instruit* [one deceives, the other enlightens].[5]) It is akin to the mental disciplines, physical exercises, and medical remedies you sometimes impose on yourself – pains subordinate to and necessary for prosperity going forward. The point is still clearer at 36:7–12:

> He does not withdraw his eyes from the righteous, but with kings upon the throne he sets them forever, and they are

exalted. And if they are bound in fetters and caught in the cords of affliction, then he declares to them their work and their transgressions, that they are behaving arrogantly. *He opens their ears to instruction* and commands that they return from iniquity. *If they hearken and serve him, they complete their days in prosperity, and their years in pleasantness. But if they do not hearken, they perish by the sword and die without knowledge.* (italics mine)

This is the sticking point for Elihu. While the friends are no doubt right in suggesting a connection between Job's suffering and his past (whether as an independent moral agent, a patriarch, or a human being), the real problem is his resistance to the very instruction that might redeem his future. In bitterness, Job turns away from what God is endeavouring to teach him. It is, by its very nature, a self-destructive rebellion:

Men of understanding will say to me, and the wise man who hears me will say: "Job speaks without knowledge, his words are without insight." Would that Job were tried to the end, because he answers like wicked men. For he adds rebellion to his sin; he claps his hands among us, and multiplies his words against God. (34:34–7)

A second precision follows directly from the first. Elihu has audited the dialogue reported in Chapters 3 to 31 closely enough to wager that Job's resistance to instruction might be assuaged by a hearing with God. Our protagonist himself says as much. Bluntly, at 13:3:

But I would speak to the Almighty, and I desire to argue my case with God.

More elaborately later in the same speech:

Behold, he will slay me; I have no hope; yet I will defend my ways to his face. This will be my salvation, that a godless man shall not come before him. Listen carefully to my words, and let my declaration be in your ears. Behold, I have prepared my case; I know that I shall be vindicated. Who is there that will contend with me? For then I would be silent and die. Only grant two things to me, then I will not hide myself from thy face: withdraw thy hand far from me, and let not dread of thee terrify me. (13:15–22)

Finally, in a deliberate contrast to "bitterness" at the beginning of Chapter 23:

Today also my complaint is bitter, his hand is heavy in spite of my groaning. Oh, that I knew where I might find him, that I might come even to his seat! I would lay my case before him and fill my mouth with arguments. I would learn what he would answer me. Would he contend with me in the greatness of his power? No: he would give heed to me. There an upright man could reason with him, and I should be acquitted forever by my judge. (23:2–7)

The friends resolutely ignore this talk, partly because Job's aspiration is in their view unimaginable (as I tried to suggest in sketching the anatomy of patience, their entrenched habit is to speak *about* God, never *to* him), but partly, in all fairness, because Job himself is so deeply ambivalent on the subject of his judicial prospects that he sometimes quails before the very thing he says he wants. Warming up the theme in Chapter 9, for example, he asks: "If it is a matter of justice, who can summon him?" then immediately laments: "Though I am innocent, my own mouth would condemn me; though I am blameless, he would prove me perverse" (9:19–20).

Elihu thinks he can remove both impediments, and so resolve the quarrel he has witnessed, with a single master stroke. He will speak explicitly *for* God. That way, Job can air his grievances honestly without the terror of facing an omnipotent being that is, to all appearances, both his accuser and his judge. But this means that the psychological condition for the possibility of giving Job his day in court – the condition for the possibility of his moving forward, of his taking instruction from suffering – is his acceptance of a kind of stand-in for the Almighty. "Answer *me*, if you can," Elihu says: "Set your words in order before *me*; take your stand. Behold I am toward God as you are; I too was formed from a piece of clay. Behold, no fear of *me* need terrify you; my pressure will not lie heavy upon you" (33:4–7, italics mine).

I'll have more to say about this crucial substitution in weighing the possible connection between Elihu and Satan, for it seems to me that there's a sense in which the Satanic, in the Book of Job and beyond it, consists always and precisely in the temptation to take simulacra for realities. Running up to that, though, I want to ponder our protagonist's non-response to Elihu's arguments (question 3 above): a second silence (that is, in addition to the weight-bearing silence reported at 2:13), the meaning of which is pivotal to grasping the import of Chapters 32 to 37, but far from obvious.

JOB'S SECOND SILENCE

Begin with the bare fact. In spite of Eluhu's offer to arbitrate Job's case (33:5–7) – indeed, in spite of his explicit call for Job's testimony (33:32) – our protagonist says nothing. He speaks neither in the course of Elihu's presentation (as he did throughout the dialogue with Eliphaz, Bildad, and Zophar) nor at its end (there is no restatement of the powerful arguments of Chapter 31, for example). Instead, he appears to take the other option Elihu gives him at 33:33: that is to say, "listen to me; be silent." Now ask yourself what interpretation of this fact advances our understanding of the narrative most effectively. Does Job's non-response mirror the friends' discomfiture, the failure to answer that Elihu belittles at 32:15–16? Is it evidence of the younger man's having redeemed the argument of his elders?

A strict reversal of positions seems unlikely. The friends "ceased to answer Job," not because they understood themselves to have been refuted, but as a result of something closer to exhaustion. They simply couldn't budge our protagonist from the conviction that he was "righteous." Job, on the other hand, is at the apex of his power and energy as the dialogue breaks off. He has answered the bell in every round of the argument, made his own name synonymous with principled resistance to theological orthodoxy. The idea that he might now be broken simply by a second barrage of that orthodoxy, that he might – still unconvinced – let Elihu's argument stand unopposed, makes nonsense of the character our author has so skilfully developed.

Is it possible, then, that Job finds Elihu convincing; that, belatedly, he's honouring the promise he made in his first response to Eliphaz – that is, "Teach me, and I will be silent" (6:24)? A definitive answer to this question would require access to our protagonist's inner life, to what his conscience was telling him about the connection between suffering and instruction. In the tradition of ancient Hebrew poetics – indeed, of ancient writing generally – our author seems determined to deny us that. But I can imagine at least two arguments, in the context of an honest self-assessment, on Elihu's behalf.

First, there's an abstract or logical sense in which the moralization of the future is incontestable. The idea that Job's suffering might be justified eventually, that it might in the fullness of time contribute to his completing his days "in prosperity," is a possibility against which he can produce no existential counter-evidence. What is to come is by definition radically open, fact-free. Whatever Job might say in response to Elihu, it can't consist simply – as in his quarrel with Eliphaz, Bildad, and Zophar – of setting his past record straight. But secondly and in any case, Job will have seen the force of something akin to Elihu's proposition in his everyday life, in the building up of his business, the raising of his family, the performance of his civic and religious duties. All of these undertakings will have presented challenges, endured through limited failures, and emerged as exemplary ("Have you considered my servant Job?") only as a result of an already-established capacity to learn from adversity. What Elihu asks our protagonist to imagine, to accept, is in some sense only the lesson of his own experience.

It's an elegant position. Not only does the younger man revisit and expand the theology of reward and punishment, he offers at the same time and by means of the same argument a rationale for endurance in adversity, something even our protagonist could not provide. The purpose of Job's suffering is instruction, improvement, wisdom. In the final analysis, the Almighty does not "pervert justice" (34:13). Even the affliction of the innocent, should such a thing actually occur, is subordinate to a greater end.

And yet, elegance notwithstanding, it seems impossible to reconcile the thought of our author's recommendation of this position with the scenes we've witnessed as a result of the complimentary backstage passes issued to us in the prologue. As appealing as the expanded theology of reward and punishment would have been for the Book of Job's original audience, for generations of its readers up into the nineteenth century – even in some respects for us – we know on the basis of Chapters 1 and 2 that it is false. I wander back in my mind to the image of J.B. intoning his sentimentally impossible trigger line at 2:6: "Behold he is in your power; only spare his life." The motivation there is neither punishment nor instruction. Job has been lauded not once but twice as "blameless and upright" (1:8, 2:3). He is presented to us explicitly – by no less an authority than the omniscient creator of the world – as a moral exemplar. In the framing encounter between God and Satan, the single thing to which our author draws attention in mythologizing the origin of suffering is the wager.

There's a third option for making sense of Job's non-response, in some ways the most natural. I touched on it in passing earlier. Our protagonist might be silent simply because the human conversation is itself overtaken by the howling of the whirlwind. Compare the transition reported at the beginning of Chapter 32 (32:1–5) with the description of the change of speakers at the beginning of 38:

So these three men ceased to answer Job, because he was righteous in his own eyes. Then Elihu the son of Barachel the Buzite, of the family of Ram, became angry. He was angry at Job because he justified himself rather than God; he was angry also at Job's three friends because they had found no answer although they had declared Job to be in the wrong. Now Elihu had waited to speak to Job because they were older than he. And when Elihu saw that there was no answer in the mouth of these three men, he became angry.

38:1 – Then the Lord answered Job out of the whirlwind.

The first passage gives you everything you need to understand the relation between the previous conversation and the one that will follow. You're told why the dialogue came to an end. The narrator makes a point of confirming the positions evident in what the interlocutors have said. The next speaker is introduced. His disdain for both parties is noted. You learn why he has waited so long to intervene, and what motivates him to do so. In contrast, the second passage marks nothing but the identity and the source of a voice. You don't know why, or even if, Elihu's sermon has reached its projected end. You're told nothing of Job's reaction. You're given neither a rationale for God's intervention nor a hint of what he will say. In short, our author provides nothing like the context he sketches in turning from the friends to Elihu. As a result, Job's epiphany arrives looking for all the world like an interruption.

Two possible interpretations of this event reframe, with respect to 38:1 in particular, the general problem of Elihu that I touched on, in passing, at the beginning of this section. The first channels something like Calvin's view: you might think of the younger man – especially qua self-appointed divine stand-in – as representing the Almighty so expertly that his auditors pass seamlessly from simulacrum to reality. The imitation of a thing – sleep, to take a mysterious but telling example from Merleau-Ponty[6] – sometimes invokes the thing itself. Someone mustering textual support for such a thesis could point to both metaphoric and discursive aspects of Chapter 37. In verses 1 to 6, for example, Elihu anticipates the voice from the whirlwind in the image of the world-forming divine word as a thunderstorm:

At this also my heart trembles, and leaps out of its place.
Hearken to the thunder of his voice and the rumbling that

comes from his mouth. Under the whole heaven he lets it go, and his lightning to the corners of the earth. After his voice roars; he thunders with his majestic voice and he does not restrain the lightnings when his voice is heard. God thunders wondrously with his voice; he does great things which we cannot comprehend. For to the snow he says, "Fall on the earth"; and to the shower and the rain, "Be strong."

A little later on, playing the stand-in more or less explicitly, he prefigures the harsh tone of cross-examination the whirlwind speeches are about to develop and amplify. Compare the tenor of Job's interrogation at 37:14–20 with the first burst of God's fury at 38:2–7.

ELIHU: Hear this, O Job; stop and consider the wondrous works of God. Do you know how God lays his command upon them, and causes the lightning of his cloud to shine? Do you know the balancings of the clouds, the wondrous works of him who is perfect in knowledge, you whose garments are hot when the earth is still because of the south wind? Can you, like him, spread out the skies, hard as a molten mirror? Teach us what we shall say to him: we cannot draw up our case because of darkness. Shall it be told him that I would speak? Did a man ever wish that he would be swallowed up? ...
GOD: Who is this that darkens counsel by words without knowledge? Gird up your loins like a man, I will question you, and you will declare to me. Where were you when I laid the foundation of the earth? Tell me, if you have understanding. Who determined its measurements – surely you know! Or who stretched the line upon it? On what were its bases sunk, or who laid its cornerstone, when the morning stars sang together, and all the sons of God shouted for joy?

Such deliberate *mimeses* prod you to see a poetic unity in Chapters 32 to 41, a single complex metaphoric/discursive gesture – what you might call a phenomenology of revelation. But if that (or anything like it) is the case, then Elihu is indeed the "organ of the spirit of God," the human face of a truth that is then repeated and developed by the Almighty himself. In this view, returning to the question at hand, Job's non-response would be merely apparent. In fact, he answers both human and divine interlocutors at 40:4–5 (where he announces the advent of his own silence) and 42:2–6 (where he confesses the error of his argument and "repents in dust and ashes"). That is to say, his final words acknowledge the power of an epiphany that begins with, and preserves as necessary, Elihu's intervention.

A second interpretation of 38:1 would channel readers like Gregory and Aquinas: You might think of Elihu as posing a problem so intractable that God has no choice but to interrupt the argument. The voice from the whirlwind here would be the original (and literal) *deus ex machina*, the divine intervention that sweeps away the mirage of human explanation. Someone mustering textual support for such a thesis would benefit greatly from taking the first question posed by God – "Who is this that darkens counsel by words without knowledge?" – as directed to Job *about* Elihu. It would then be possible to interpret the command that follows – "Gird up your loins like a man, I will question you, and you shall answer" – as insistence on the intimacy of unmediated address and response I proposed earlier as the foundation of Job's patience.

It is as if God were saying: "To hell with the stand-in! What's at stake here can be sorted only between you and me!" On the issue of why the Almighty takes this view in spite of the metaphoric and discursive resemblances between Elihu's speech and the one he's about to make, you might point again, at least in beginning to elaborate an argument, to the counter-evidence of the prologue. The already-manifest problem with Elihu's simulacrum is that its account of Job's suffering is untrue. In the spirit of this experiment, you might then continue to take our protagonist's non-response as evidence of his having been swayed or at least shaken by Elihu. His silence, here, would be read as provoking an interruption designed to prevent Job from surrendering a position that is both theologically and phenomenologically superior to those of his interlocutors.

ELIHU AND SATAN

These readings seem diametrically opposed. According to the first, Elihu is a faithful mirror of divine will, the beginning of a story God himself takes up and brings to an end; according to the second, he is an intolerable forgery. Still – and for me this is absolutely essential – they have something important in common: the idea of Elihu as simulacrum, as stand-in for the Almighty. I want to develop this idea now, picking up the thread of a suggestion I left hanging in question 2, by customizing the Talmudic suggestion that Elihu represents the return of Satan – that is, by responding to question 4.

Come back with me to the living tableau of the Blake engraving at the end of Peter's scene study in the little black-box theatre. Imagine our actors frozen in place, so that you and I can circle them in memory once, twice, even three times if necessary. Look at the figures stage left, human faces displayed to the audience, Satanic half-masks turned away. In the original work, as you know, Blake meant to represent only Eliphaz, Bildad, and Zophar. In the thought experiment we're about to perform, you need to see Elihu's face here as well (the way you see the origin of a child's face sometimes in the faces of older relatives). If what I said in responding to questions 2 and 3 above is plausible, he is both the mirror and the development of the theology of reward and punishment, the proverbial next generation.

Follow me onto the stage now. I want to get behind what I saw at the end of the performance. There's just enough room for us to walk through the middle of the scene – between Job and his friends. Don't go directly upstage, though. Stop instead on the hypothetical line that separates front and back. Linger for a moment in Job's place, staring down these characters – half-human, half-divine – pointing at us now their fingers of accusation. Accusation, as it turns out, is key to the cast of mind our author wants to portray, both in Satan and in the entire troupe of human comforters. Indeed, a little reflection on what you might call its epistemic preconditions brings out vividly at least one scenario for reading Elihu as Satan's double, as his proverbial final word.

With this in mind, take three steps upstage now and look at the scene from the back. The first thing of note, so obvious as to be almost invisible, is that the accusers set themselves apart from the accused. There is a distance that the pointing fingers make evident. The plastic and dramatic arts capture it immediately, because they work with bodies in space. But the poetry and prose of the Book of Job – mediated, of course, by language and its operations – also present Satan, Eliphaz, Bildad, Zophar, and Elihu self-consciously as creatures of distance. Satan's summary of his own activities in the prologue – "going to and fro on the earth, and ... walking up and down on it" – give him an air of objectivity, as if he were the original anthropologist, a proto-Mead or Levi-Strauss, a stranger in a strange land, observing its customs and values. What he provides to God as a run up to their original wager is a kind of field report ("Job, yes, interesting case – but let's control for material prosperity; it's obviously colouring your judgment"). Even his predictions of Job's reaction ("he's going to curse you") have a kind of laboratory air – as if based on a general hypothesis rather than intimate knowledge of Job qua individual ("my studies suggest the following reaction to loss of cattle, household, and children as absolutely typical"). In short, he is detached, and from the perspective produced precisely by that detachment, offers God what he takes to be the whole picture with respect to the human condition.

Here already there is a simulacrum. In the spirit of anthropology, Satan represents what he takes to be the principles that govern our words and deeds. The tribe and its possibilities embodied by Job in the prologue become images of his anthropologists' objectivity. Now come round again to the front of the tableau and examine its human faces. You see the same moments. The theology of reward and punishment, in both its initial and expanded forms, presupposes the transcendence of human experience. To speak about or for God as creator of the universe is to take up a position in front of the life we actually live, to stand outside of it, to have it as an object. This object too is a representation, a simulacrum. Eliphaz, Bildad, Zophar, and Elihu are able to interpret Job's situation and his prospects, to make sense of his suffering, to accuse him of impiety and rebelliousness, only because they imagine before them a comprehensive map of human possibility.

But the picture-thinking of representation isn't the only trigger of the accusation levelled at Job. Follow me upstage again. I want to point out a feature of Satanic detachment that sets it apart from other modes of reflection. It's on display in the first response to God's praise of our protagonist at 1:9–11:

> Does Job fear God for nought? Hast thou not put a hedge about him and his house and all that he has, on every side? Thou hast blessed the work of his hands, and his possessions have increased in the land. But put forth thy hand now, and touch all that he has, and he will curse thee to thy face.

Satan's anthropology is, as it turns out, a (very early) species of behaviourism. The principle essential to comprehending human action is that of stimulus/response. On this view, Job's piety is neither a marker of his own integrity nor an expression of genuine religious devotion. It is simply the by-product of a pleasant environment, a response to positive stimuli ("Thou hast blessed the work of his hands, and his possessions have increased in the land"). If, in the spirit of experiment, God reverses things – if Job's environment is made manifestly unpleasant, if the stimuli are negative – the mirage of personal integrity will vanish ("But put forth thy hand now, and touch all that he has, and he will curse thee to thy face"). The world of human words and deeds is a set of explainable behaviours, a compendium of responses to pleasure and pain. Praise of Job – or anyone else – as a free and dignified moral agent is simply naive.

Is that the view downstage as well? At the outset of the dialogue, Eliphaz especially sounds like the God of 1:8 and 2:3, celebrating the dignity of the moral hero ("Is not the fear of God your confidence, and the integrity of your ways your hope?"). But as comfort hardens into ideology, the friends' God looks more and more like a practitioner of behaviour modification, more and more a professor of Satan-style anthropology. The good, as they conceive it, he conditions in us by means of reward, the evil he purges by means of punishment. Here you have positive and negative stimuli by another name, controlled and operationalized at the level of the cosmos. And all human fortune and misfortune, no matter how evidently mysterious or apparently undeserved, reduces – in terms of this big picture – to one or the other.

Satan shares with Job's human interlocutors, then, a basic representation of the human condition, the frame of which is broadly behaviouristic: God vouchsafes the difference between good and evil here below by dispensing rewards and punishments. Such a representation sanctions naturally the accusation of those who suffer. It follows directly from apprehension of the basic sense of the world. But now – coming to the point of the present experiment – what about Elihu in particular? Why single him out as Satan's double or take his argument as Satan's final word? Let's do one more round of the tableau. You're here in a position to see what I take to be decisive both for the Satan/Elihu relation and for the movement of Job himself round back of the ironies in which, qua sufferer, he is initially lost.

Imagine again that "second day" reported in the prologue. Satan has put Job to the test only to have his behaviourism confounded – "In all this Job did not sin or charge God with wrong," our narrator says (1:22). To which, as you've seen, God himself adds, "He still holds fast his integrity, although you moved me against him, to destroy him without cause" (2:3). Now, weigh Satan's options, not this time as if he were playing in a *Pride and Prejudice*-style comedy of manners, but granting him the prestige due his present role as the original social scientist. He could have been magnanimous: "You're right. There's something in Job, in the human condition itself, for which I've failed to account." Or, channelling Immanuel Kant (the philosophical holdings of the eternal library are comprehensive), he could have modified the ontological claims of his science: "How things might *be* with specific individuals notwithstanding, it remains best to act *as if* human action were governed by reward and punishment." But he doesn't do either of these things. Instead, in an act of hubris that would tempt virtually every subsequent theorist, he doubles down on his original conviction, determined to make the messy chaos of human reality disappear into the simplicity of his representation. The experiment must be radicalized, the source of the recalcitrant evidence must itself be attacked, degraded. Where everything – including the living body – has been reduced to negative stimuli, surely even Job will confirm the original hypothesis: "Skin for skin! All that a man has he will give for his life. But put forth thy hand now, and touch his bone and his flesh, and he will curse thee to thy face" (2:4–5).

Satan's story comes to this: if he is to be vindicated, the frontiers of his own imagination must be extended to the point where they encompass the world entirely; to the point where there is no difference between human experience and the simulacrum he proposes. Now follow me downstage one more time. In just this respect, Elihu is Satan's double. The theology of reward and punishment he inherits from Eliphaz, Bildad, and Zophar has been breached by Job's "integrity" in precisely the way Satan's original prediction is confounded. And, as in the prologue, it must be restored – vindicated – by means of radicalization. Elihu accomplishes that radicalization by widening the scope of negative reinforcement to include instruction. Suffering not only punishes, it educates. It is not only retribution for past behaviour, but redemption of the future. But that means: In Elihu's expansion of the friends' theology, the economy of reward and punishment encompasses all human experience. His argument is the repetition – indeed, the perfection – of the prologue's Satanism. From this perspective, you may read the second precision of the friends' argument – the advocacy Elihu offers Job, the invitation to present his case – as sealing the wilful eclipse of the real by its simulacrum. Even the voice of God is here appropriated by the human imagination: "Answer *me*, if you can," he exhorts our protagonist at 33:5, "set your words before *me*" (italics mine). In a manner he does not anticipate, Job's worst fear is realized. His accuser has become his judge.

THE SPECTRAL AND THE REAL

I want to suggest to you that, for our author, Satan is first and foremost a name for the hubris of imagination. In the prologue, this hubris provokes the wager. It produces the origin of suffering. In the dialogue, it carries Job's human interlocutors from solidarity to accusation, from compassion to condemnation to rage. Finally, in the Elihu chapters, it eclipses the voice of the Almighty itself. The danger of such a substitution seems, on the one hand, hard to grasp. You would think that, in contrast to the presence of the real, of what is, the simulacra of the imagination would be spectral, no more tempting as a stand-in for the things themselves than a cardboard cutout or a statue at Madame Tussaud's wax museum. But, on the other hand, such simulacra are indispensable to human accommodation. Neither the refuge of personal history nor the refuge of universality is possible without them. And though we do not always impose on ourselves the methodological rigour of anthropology or psychology, there is not a day – perhaps not even a moment – when we don't stand in some degree outside our experience, beholding it like a picture. The transcendent imagination is an indispensable component of human self-consciousness. Paradoxically that means: its spectres are essential.

Here is a way of reconciling the contending impressions of Elihu that I mentioned at the outset: he embodies the Satanic eclipse of the real by the self-constituting spectres of the imagination. Or again, responding directly to the terms of question 5 above: his being, the literary reflection of our own indispensable hubris, our author presents to us as both spectral and essential.

Here is a way of reconciling the contending interpretations of Job's non-response: it marks the moment that comes even to the patient, even to those capable of faith and prayer, where our longing for steadfast accommodation, our natural desire to make ourselves at home in the world, tempts us to take simulacra for reality – when, knowing we are dreaming, we wish to dream on; willing, in effect, our own delusion.

There's a chapter near the end of Dostoevsky's *The Brothers Karamazov* that develops brilliantly one resolution of this moment.

The middle son, Ivan Fyodorovich, a pamphleteer for the new materialism, has fallen ill and teeters on the brink of madness. Having long ago banished God from the world, he is unpleasantly surprised to find himself stuck with Satan, a social-climbing mooch in a cheap suit, who imposes on his hospitality and bores him with tedious rationalizations of his activity as an agent of historical mayhem. A kind of social hell, no doubt. But the most terrifying thing about this residue of Christian orthodoxy, from Ivan's own perspective, is his lack of independent reality: "in yourself you do not exist," he screams at one point. "You are *me*, all you are is *myself*, and nothing more! You are rubbish, you are my imagination!"[7] Our author's logic is here extended into the godless world of post-Enlightenment Russia. The devil, there as in the Book of Job, is absolutely unfettered human imagination. Dostoevsky doesn't withhold judgment on this mode of being. In the world that gathers round it "everything is permitted," and if you take Ivan Fyodorovich as its exemplar, its final station is madness.

In another poem – perhaps (I say it sadly) in a contemporary phenomenology of suffering – Job might have been Brother Ivan. He might have resolved the moment our author deliberately suspends in his non-response by giving himself completely to the labour of imagination,[8] or by renouncing that labour entirely and descending into complete incoherence. It seems far more like what might happen now. But the sentimental brands of optimism and pessimism (the sufferer learns a lesson, the sufferer is broken down and shattered) that dominate the philosophy and literature of the post-Enlightenment are but spectral possibilities of the future in ancient Uz. Our author feels no obligation to choose between them. He's after something grander, something far more poetically ambitious. The journey of his protagonist must culminate, head uncovered, heart open, in the awesome storm of the real.

7

The Voice from the Whirlwind

THE LESSONS OF SEQUENCE

At a university function several years ago now, I was catching up with a friend I hadn't seen over the course of the summer. He makes his living in communications, but had studied theology with George Grant in the late 1970s. We'd talked from time to time about the precarious state of contemporary philosophy and the challenges facing liberal education. I admired his determination, while sitting on our board of governors, to keep these disciplines from falling completely off the agenda of academic and strategic planning. When, following the established pattern of our conversations, he asked me what I'd been reading, I said with some enthusiasm: "The Book of Job – in particular, God's speeches 'out of the whirlwind.'" He looked at me, eyes narrowing slightly, for two or three seconds. Then, with that odd mix of relief and apprehension characteristic of someone making a confession, said simply: "Disappointing, eh?"

At that point on the first leg of my own odyssey as a student of Chapters 38 to 41, I laughed in recognition. It was an honest description of my experience as well. What I've learned since is that for many readers – perceptive and fully engaged – the disappointment is insurmountable. As far back as the 1930s, the Norwegian theologian Peter Wessel Zapffe had argued that meeting God, Job:

finds himself confronted with a world ruler of grotesque primitiveness, a cosmic cave-dweller, a braggart and blusterer, almost agreeable in his total ignorance of spiritual culture ... What is new for Job is not God's greatness in quantifiable terms; that he knew fully in advance ... What is new is the qualitative baseness.[1]

Elaborating on Zapffe's position in support of his own analysis, the philosopher Slavoj Žižek adds:

In other words, God – the God of the *Rea* – is *das Ding*, a capricious cruel master who simply has no sense of universal justice.[2]

Even Elie Wiesel, for whom Job himself remains a "contemporary" – "seen on every road of Europe" after the unprecedented devastation of the Second World War – finds only empty abstractions in his culminating epiphany:

Actually, God said nothing that Job could interpret as an answer or an explanation or a justification of his ordeals. God did not say: You sinned, you did wrong. Nor did He admit His own error. He dealt in generalities, offering nothing but vast simplifications.[3]

It is an indictment that bleeds, eventually, into the assessment of our author's guardianship of the narrative:

It seems rather odd that the Midrash, so prodigal in legends at the beginning of the drama, becomes so sparing in its epilogue; it probably troubled the rabbinical storytellers. The third act of a play is usually a kind of apotheosis; this one is pale, disappointing. The fighter has turned into a lamb. A sad metamorphosis, inexplicable in literary terms.[4]

Wiesel's final claim, especially, frames what I take to be our hermeneutical challenge. Is it, in fact, impossible to read Chapters 38 to 41 as anything but a betrayal of the character developed so convincingly in the dialogue, a compromise of the integrity for which Job is so justly celebrated, a botched ending? Or do God's speeches provide an indispensable supplement to the text's human voices; the moment in our projected phenomenology where Job finds himself qua sufferer, where experience issues him at last the backstage pass we readers have had since the prologue, where he sees the truth of his condition?

Needless to say, *I* want the second option. But here, as never before, you must mitigate your first impressions of the voice that delivers it. It's easy enough to find traces of Job's human interlocutors on the map of your own relations with others: you've been touched, no doubt, from time to time, by something like his wife's exasperation, or the youthful exuberance of Elihu's interruption. Part of our author's genius lies in articulating a cast of characters in which you may recognize yourself. On the other hand, almost nothing understandably, endearingly, or forgivably human remains in the speeches from the whirlwind. The words themselves howl unremittingly, and your modern ear, bombarded already by the post-Enlightenment choruses of religious disenchantment, can't help but hear in their inhumanness, at least initially, some violation of the humane values rightly articulated as fundamental by the institutions of the modern world (that is, some form of "qualitative baseness"). How then might you listen for something else?

Defer, for a moment, the assessment of *what* God says to Job. Content seems to be the sticking point for disappointed readers. Look first, instead, at what a colleague of mine would call the scene's "sequence."[5] If we take our protagonist's final words as a transition to the epilogue, it comprises essentially two speeches. The first runs from the sudden onset of the storm at 38:1 ("Who is this that darkens counsel by words without knowledge") to the demand of a counterargument at 40:2 ("Shall a faultfinder contend with the Almighty? He who argues with God, let him answer it"); the second runs from the resumption of the diatribe at 40:7 ("Gird up your loins like a man; I will question you, and you declare to me") to the final stanzas of the extraordinary hymn to the Leviathan at 41:33–4 ("Upon the earth there is not his like, a creature without fear. He beholds everything that is high; he is king over all the sons of pride"). Between the two you find a mere three verses – the sum of Job's dialogue in the entire passage:

> Then Job answered the Lord: "Behold, I am of small account; what shall I answer thee? I lay my hand on my mouth. I have spoken once, and I will not answer; twice, but I will proceed no further." (40:3–5)

This is the beginning of Wiesel's "sad metamorphosis," the transition from "fighter" to "lamb." But resonating here there's also an important echo of what you might call Job's original condition, which seems to me decisive for understanding the role God's speeches play in the drama of the work as a whole. What is it?

Cast your mind back to the thought experiment we devised when attempting to untangle the apparent contradiction of Job's initial interventions (1:21, 2:10, 3:3). In it, you were an actor charged with bringing our protagonist to life in the opening scenes of his drama. What you discovered, in search of a compelling performance, was that the wordless communion with Eliphaz, Bildad, and Zophar (2:13) constituted a discursive centre of gravity that pulled on – that pulled apart – the spoken words in orbit around it. In the draw of Job's original silence, you could hear the despair pouring out of his proto-Stoicism ("the Lord gave, and the Lord has taken away"); you could hear the persistence rising out of his nihilism ("let the day perish wherein I was born"). Those same movements we then found again, repeated, in the wider orbit of the dialogue. By the time we arrived at the third cycle of speeches, we could see the friends' rage pouring out of their reason. By the time we worked through the articles of the code of behaviour Job elaborates in Chapter 28, we could see his patience arising from the restless contradiction of his bitterness. One way or another, virtually every proposition, from the moment Job opens his mouth in the prologue to the point at which Eliphaz, Bildad, and Zophar "cease to answer" him at the beginning of Chapter 32 seemed subject to – shaped by – the gravity of the silence described at 2:13.

But if that is the case, then 40:3–5 reports a gesture of tremendous significance. "I lay my hand on my mouth," Job says. That is "I return now, not helplessly or passively, not in the grip of some irony invisible to me, but intentionally and knowingly, to the sheltering dignity of wordlessness." "I enact, in the explicit renunciation of speech, the return to silence already implied in Elihu's unmet challenge to speak at 33:32–3." It's as if all the elements of the drama – its poetry, its characters, its arguments, its misapprehensions and reversals, the force of its eventual epiphany – conspire finally to take our protagonist behind his original human reticence to explicit apprehension of the ineffable. As if our author, having traced and retraced the movements of pouring out and arising that run together in suffering against the backdrop of the Satanic imagination and the pilgrimage of patience, now lays over the mute passion of Job's fall from grace the transparency of a cultivated, self-conscious silence – as Euripides lays the sacrificial death of Polyxena over the bloody murder of Polydorus in the *Hecuba*, as Kafka lays the voice of the court over that of the risen Christ in the priest's address of Joseph K. at the dramatic climax of *The Trial*. "As if," I say, but I myself find the prospect of a return to silence, a doubling of silence, a phenomenology of suffering stretching from the unbidden descent of silence to its truth, irresistible. In a poem where every word is weighed and measured, and where – from the prologue onward – the conceit, consistently, is to take us behind the facades of language, how could our protagonist's deliberate renunciation of the word in the eye of his stormy encounter with God be anything other than structurally and philosophically central? How could Job's final interventions, here and in transition to the epilogue (42:1–6), be anything other than the proverbial other shoe dropping, the second point at which our author's linguistic sculpture makes contact with the ground?

What follows from this hypothesis? Among other things, returning now to the lessons of sequence: a question about the speeches on either side of 40:3–5. What if God's sermons (38:1 to 40:2, 40:7 to 41:34) were subject to the gravitational pull of Job's final silence in the same way Job's initial interventions (1:21,

2:10, 3:3) are subject to the gravitational pull of the first? Or to be more specific: What if you were to discover in God's first speech the truth of the event you grasped originally as despair pouring out of proto-Stoicism, and in God's second speech the truth of the event you grasped originally as persistence arising out of nihilism? In that circumstance, Chapters 38 to 41 would amount to a re-presentation of Chapters 1:21 to 3:3, pointing simultaneously both at what is backstage of Job's stoicism/ despair, behind his nihilism/persistence, and to the space between mute passion and deliberate renunciation that accommodates the entirety of his experience "put to the test." And the lesson of our phenomenology would be that in suffering – the path from one silence to another – all propositions are ironic, markers of a draw, pointers that *with*draw, like rungs of the philosophical ladder Wittgenstein encourages his readers to throw away, having climbed it, at the end of the *Tractatus.*[6]

"REALITY POINT BLANK"

In what sense, then, and to what extent is it possible to imagine 38:1 to 40:2 as the truth of the event you grasped originally as despair pouring out of proto-Stoicism? In what would this truth – as a truth – consist? I want to begin by reminding you that your object here is itself dynamic. You want to grasp the moment the heart sinks in spite of the tongue's calm assurance, the moment uncontainable sadness breaches the defence of reason, the moment external forces invade the experience you conceive as yours alone. You want to grasp the draw of existential dispossession, of abandonment. This phenomenon surfaced for you as you tried to make dramatic sense of the scene that runs between 1:21 and 3:3. But it appeared there in negative space, an effect of what you might call the triangulation of Stoicism, nihilism, and silence.

In the transition from Chapter 37 to Chapter 38, this valence is reversed. The event of dispossession/abandonment, specifically as a breach of the moral imagination, is represented positively. The medium of the transition is the meteorological image. At 37:21, having extended the domain of the theology of reward and punishment to the very limit of temporality, Elihu concludes:

> And now men cannot look on the light when it is bright in the skies, *when the wind has passed and cleared them*. Out of the north comes golden splendor; God is clothed with terrible majesty. The Almighty – we cannot find him; he is great in power and justice, and abundant righteousness he will not violate. Therefore men fear him; he does not regard any who are wise in their own conceit. (37:23–24, italics mine)

Our author then writes simply, bluntly, and immediately at 38:1: "Then the Lord answered Job *out of the whirlwind*" (italics mine).

From the clear blue sky of Elihu's imagination, then – the sudden real and irreconcilable storm of God's word! Here you need not feel your way to what T.S. Eliot calls the "slip, slide," and "perish"[7] of discursive simulacra by means of an exercise in acting, as if Job's despair were a fleeting tone or a shadow of something inexpressible. The whirlwind itself voices – *embodies* – the draw of Job's original silence. It is the concrete Other of human reason; all movement – sinking, breaching, invading. In Chapters 38 to 42, God speaks *as* the fury of the whirlwind. The manner in which our author chooses to voice the speeches of the Almighty is as important to grasping their role in the drama of the Book of Job as their sequence. Fury, as it turns out, is itself a mode of disclosure that conditions in advance all content. What does it reveal?

Time for the aid from Henry Bugbee I promised in spinning out the daydream of my interview with our author as a warm-up to reflecting on patience. Near the end of *The Inward Morning*, he tells a story from his own life that is, in important respects, an epitome of Job's experience. In addition to answering the question I posed just now, it doubles the transition from calm to storm that brings fury onstage – starting at 38:2. I cite it in full:

> It was in the summertime, at a summer resort, along the
> North Fork of the Trinity River in California, on a day like

so many summer days of bright sun streaming down through the tops of the pines. Most of the length and breadth of that long, smooth, flowing pool lay translucently exposed to the bouldered bottom. Children played on the sandy shores, or splashed along the fringes of the pool. The air was of ambient fragrance of pines, reassuring warmth and stillness, refreshing coolness of moving water, and frank with the murmur of conversation punctuated by shouts of farthest remove from alarm. The roar of the rapids below the pool might have been but a ground-bass of contentment, filling us all.

There came a cry for help, seconded with a cry of fright, and I turned toward the tail of the pool just in time to see a young man desperately, failingly, clinging to a great log which had been chained as a boom across the lower end (to raise the water level in the pool). No one could reach him in time. An enormous suction under the log had firm hold of the greater part of his body and drew him ineluctably under. He bobbed to the surface of the first great wave of the rapid below, but there was no swimming or gaining the bottom to stay what seemed an impending execution on the rocks at the bend in this mill-race, some hundred yards on down. But it chanced that the river was abnormally high, and as it carried this helpless man doomward it swept him just for an instant under the extremity of a willow which arched far out from the bank and erratically trailed its branch-tips on the heaving waters. With a wild clutch the young man seized a gathering of the supple branches and held. Everything held, that firm grip and that rooted willow, while the rush of the river brought him in an arc downstream and to the bank. He had barely the strength and the breath to claw himself up the muddy slope onto firmament.

I had run across the log and arrived on the opposite side below the willow, where he now paused, panting and on all fours, unable to rise. Slowly he raised his head and we looked into each other's eyes. I lifted out both hands and helped him to his feet. Not a word passed between us. As nearly as I can relive the matter, the compassion I felt with this man gave way

into awe and respect for what I witnessed in him. He seemed
absolutely clean. In that steady gaze of his I met reality point
blank, filtered and distilled as the purity of a man.

   I think of Meister Eckhart's "becoming as we were before
we were born." I think of what Conrad says of the storms
visited on sailors far at sea as chastening them. I think, too,
of Camus' remark at the close of *The Stranger* about a
woman in her last moments of life before death: "No one,
no one in the world had any right to weep for her."[8]

This story contains, for me, at least four insights relevant to
interpreting 38:1 to 40:2. There is first a simple, but very powerful, answer to the question of what fury reveals. It comes in the
final sentence of the penultimate paragraph, as Bugbee recollects
explicitly what he saw – what he discovered – in the face of the
unnamed man swallowed and disgorged by the "heaving waters"
of the river: "In that steady gaze of his I met *reality point blank*."
That is to say: not a theory or conjecture, not a hypothesis or an
imaginative construction, not a simulacrum, but what *is* as such.
The violence of nature casts you into the midst of the real in a
way you cannot possibly anticipate from the safety of your
established accommodations. Bugbee's man, our protagonist, all
those swallowed and disgorged by suffering, show us that terrible intimacy. They have been touched by the unmediated revelation of an existence that is, in truth, wild, chaotic, and bereft
of compassion.

   The revelation of existence Bugbee meets in his unnamed
man's "steady gaze" gives you something like a template for
grasping our author's representation of God's word. This would
be the second point. Although there is a logic governing the
speeches from the whirlwind, they are not first and foremost
abstract arguments of the kind we saw in the cycles of the dialogue or the Elihu chapters. On the contrary, they make discursive the overwhelming power of nature. You need to see Job
pulled into this tempest the way Bugbee's man is pulled into the
current of the river – flailing impotently against the limits of his
own agency. And correlatively: you need to grasp God's word as

irresistible, not because it addresses convincingly the moral questions of previous episodes, but because it sweeps all such questions away. Here is the first step in dealing with Wiesel's disappointment in particular. It would have been senseless for Bugbee's man to object to the river's current on moral grounds. For the same reason, you can't expect Job, post-38:1, to persist either in his general recalcitrance or his specific demand of the right to cross-examination. He may have dreamed originally of hailing God into court. But his epiphany, when it comes, is a storm.

Here I imagine the following objection: Meteorological images notwithstanding, you see the unsurpassed trace of moral discourse at the climax of both these narratives. Bugbee says of his protagonist, "[h]e seemed absolutely clean" – a representation of reality "filtered and distilled as the purity of a man." The encounter then brings to mind "what Conrad says of the storms visited on sailors far at sea as chastening them." The final statement our author gives to Job runs: "I had heard of thee by the hearing of the ear, but now my eyes see thee, therefore I despise myself, and repent in dust and ashes" (42:5–6). Mustn't you acknowledge in each case the perception of a pilgrimage from "worse" to "better" – of an Elihu-style instruction in suffering? And, as regards Job specifically, doesn't this pilgrimage frame precisely the disappointing transition from "fighter" to "lamb"?

I would reply: The unstated premise of such an argument is that all modes of purification and repentance are moral. But that's precisely what's at issue. What if Bugbee's point were that his companion's terrifying baptism constitutes a supra-moral purification? What if the outcome of our author's phenomenology of suffering were that moral discourse, while indispensable to the account of our condition, nevertheless fails to compass in its own terms the most profound and transformative repentance? "What if," I say – but that's how it is.

This would be the third point. Writing out of the existential/phenomenological tradition, Bugbee wants to illustrate for you what Heidegger calls Being-towards-death – the experience in which the meaning of your radical finitude becomes forcefully present. The unnamed man is "absolutely clean," in the sense that the river has washed out of him the everyday accommodations that would have obscured and tranquilized that meaning prior to his moment of crisis; "chastened," because he has grasped in no uncertain terms the difference between simulacra and reality. His purification is ontological. The promise to "repent in dust and ashes" that our author puts in Job's mouth needs to be read in the same spirit. What our protagonist recognizes there is the failure of his own bitterness, that is, of his pining for a moral explanation that cannot be given. Repentance is necessary not because Job sees, at last, that his suffering was warranted or that his despair was illusory, but because the *reality* of these things is distorted by the facade of language in general, and of his own moral language in particular. In bitterness, Job voices the incommensurability of his personal history with the "universal justice" that is held out to him in the theology of reward and punishment as an intolerable – unnatural – contradiction. But this contradiction – God's destruction of "both the blameless and the wicked" (9:22), his crushing of Job himself "with a tempest" (9:17) – turns out to be the most natural thing in the world, the truth of nature, of existence itself.

Finally, if language in general and moral language in particular distort what fury reveals, then accounts dedicated to representing its content faithfully ought to draw you toward silence, a wordlessness that acknowledges as a constitutive ground of your experience the breach of the transcendent imagination, the invasion of a primordial and ontologically determinative external force. And this, of course, you see both in the culmination of the story from *The Inward Morning* and at the crucial hinge of Job's epiphany. Recounting the precise moment of his encounter with the unnamed man, Bugbee writes:

> Slowly he raised his head and we looked into each other's eyes. I lifted out both hands and helped him to his feet. *Not a word passed between us.* As nearly as I can relive the matter, the compassion I felt with this man gave way into awe and respect for what I witnessed in him. (Italics mine)

Apprehending what is revealed to him in the divine fury of the whirlwind, Job says, returning to where I began in this reflection:

Behold, I am of small account; what shall I answer thee? *I lay my hand upon my mouth*. I have spoken once, and I will not answer; twice, but I will proceed no further. (italics mine)

So – thinking through the sequence-position of 38:1 to 40:2, you come to the Euripides-inspired hypothesis that our author effectively lays God's speech over the emotional trajectory of Job's proto-Stoicism in order to expose its truth; thinking through its discursive form, to the Bugbee-inspired hypothesis that that truth is "reality point blank," or existence. Moreover, you see that both Job's uncomprehended despair and the discovery of its source or truth draw him toward silence – in the first case as the inchoate prelude to moral outrage and justification, in the second as the marker of its limit. If you turn now from form to content, to what extent can you imagine this argument extended and strengthened?

THE LOGIC OF FINITUDE

Reviewing what God *says* at your leisure, you are, of course, in a position virtually the opposite of Job's. He is the proverbial man in the river, overcome by the storm, grasping at any lifeline. You (I mean you as reader) are far more like the observer Kant describes in connection with the dynamically sublime.[9] Nature's might stimulates your imagination in the safety of the armchair by the window of your living room. What you see, from that vantage point, is already a quiet image of the wild reality I've tried to evoke in relation to the story from *The Inward Morning*. I want to repeat here what I said at the beginning of my look at the discourses of the comforters: Our author calls on you consistently to pierce such images, to apprehend in all arguments a kind of movement in stasis. God's *logos*, the content of his speech, needs ultimately to serve its form. It is a series of propositions designed to evoke the howling of the whirlwind, a ladder to be thrown away in the process of comprehending its force. Bearing this in mind, consider how the speech begins:

> Who is this that darkens counsel by words without knowledge? Gird up your loins like a man, I will question you, and you shall declare to me. Where were you when I laid the foundation of the earth? Tell me, if you have understanding. Who determined its measurements – surely you know! Or who stretched the line upon it? On what were its bases sunk, or who laid its cornerstone, when the morning stars sang together, and all the sons of God shouted for joy? (32:2–7)

God makes two things evident straight away. First, the tables will be turned completely on our protagonist's idea of a day in court (13:3, 13:15–22, 23:2–7). It is not God who will be cross-examined, but Job himself (as in the old story of the undergraduate who provokes the ire of his elderly professor by offering a criticism of *Hamlet*: "Mr So-and-so, Shakespeare's not on trial here. *You* are!") Under the pressure of this cross-examination, Job will wilt. The questions are impossible. You know in a matter of seconds that they are posed for rhetorical effect, that no human being could ever have responded to them successfully. And you see, in any case, that answers are beside the point. God's interrogation of Job is an expression of his overwhelming might – a reflection of the ontology suggested in Bugbee's story. Job's boundless ignorance is an image of his flailing in the storm.

Secondly, the object of the Almighty's interest in the role of prosecutor will be nothing less than creation itself, the process by means of which "reality point blank," or existence, gets hammered together. As his line of questioning unfolds, what is essential to that process emerges with surprising clarity. Consider three representative passages. Picking up the text, first at 38:8:

> Or who shut in the sea with doors, when it burst forth from the womb; when I made clouds its garment and thick darkness its swaddling band, and prescribed bounds for it, and set

bars and doors, and said, "Thus far shall you come and no farther, and here shall your proud waves be stayed?"

Add to this the text that runs from verses 16 to 18 of the same chapter:

Have you entered into the springs of the sea, or walked in the recesses of the deep? Have the gates of death been revealed to you, or have you seen the gates of deep darkness? Have you comprehended the expanse of the earth? Declare if you know all this.

Finally, look at the foray into astronomy, 38:31–3:

Can you bind the chains of the Pleiades, or loose the cords of Orion? Can you lead forth the Mazzaroth in their season, or can you guide the Bear with its children? Do you know the ordinances of the heavens? Can you establish their rule on the earth?

What is fundamental to creation in all these cases is something like the imposition of limit. The Almighty presses the fury of existence into the places he allots to things (their dwellings, their homes, compare 38:19–20) and holds it fast there. He has the power to "shut in the sea with doors," to "prescribe bounds," to "set bars," to forge "the gates of death," to "bind the chains" of constellations, to establish "ordinances" and inaugurate "rules." Creation, in Chapter 38, is determination, negation. Its constitutive act is a making-finite, a harnessing of precisely the force that has Job in its grasp, that overpowers everything and everyone except God himself.

But – and this is key – if the act of creation is a pressing into place, a defining of limit, then it is simultaneously also an exposure of things determined at that limit. A created thing, as created, is open to the fury of existence excluded from it in and by its very creation. Call it the logic of finitude. I am reminded of the single axiom Spinoza gives you at the beginning of *Ethics*

4. It expresses this thought with characteristic economy: "There is in Nature no individual thing that is not surpassed in strength and power by some other thing. Whatsoever thing there is, there is another more powerful by which the said thing can be destroyed."[10]

Here you come to the ontological foundation of what I've been trying to think about since the beginning of this reflection under the heading of indifference. The logic of finitude, of "shutting doors" and "setting bars," of forging "gates," establishing "ordinances," and inaugurating "rules" – of creation as limitation – itself entails the abandonment of things created. To make something finite is to leave it unprotected at the place where it breaks off and ceases to be. Or again: Indifference to the possibility of a thing's destruction is the price of its creation. In the terrifying moments at which you meet "reality point blank," existence as such, the trade-off becomes abundantly clear.

This ontology is not simply implicit in the images of Chapter 38. It is itself elaborated in the second part of the speech, precisely in terms of the contrast between love and indifference with which I began (reflecting on the lessons of Plato and Heidegger, Euripides and Kafka). In Chapter 39, our author supplements God's catalogue of limits with a description of the modalities of existence that follow from it. Gearing up for the encomium to monsters (Behemoth and Leviathan) that dominates Chapters 40 and 41, he draws his material now from the animal kingdom. At 39:13, he turns to the case of the ostrich and her young, offering what I take to be a description of life as it is in reality – that is, unmediated by the transcendent imagination in general and the theology of reward and punishment in particular.

The wings of the ostrich wave proudly; but are they the pinions and plumage of love? For she leaves her eggs on the earth, and lets them be warmed by the ground, forgetting that a foot may crush them, and that a wild beast may trample them. She deals cruelly with her young, as if they were not hers; though her labour be in vain, yet she has no fear; because God has made her forget wisdom, and given her no share in understanding. When she rouses herself to flee, she laughs at the horse and his rider. (39:13–18)

Beyond the distinctively human capacities for wisdom and under-standing – in our protagonist's terms, beyond "the fear of the Lord," the "departure from evil," and the tension between the two – there is no resistance to the divine indifference that appears so incomprehensible in the Book of Job's opening scene. It is the way of nature, dictated by and harmonious with finitude itself. The ostrich has no concern for the "pinions and plumage" of sentimental love. What she "knows" is the directive of creation. She gives her young unprotected to the world, where they may be warmed or trampled. The wager of her action is that her fecun-dity – her persistence in the business of life – will prevail against the ineluctable possibility of destruction.

I flash back to the theological climax of Peter's adaptation of the prologue. The Satan stage left has just bet the house: "[P]ut forth thy hand now, and touch his bone and his flesh, and he will curse thee to thy face." I imagine again J.B.'s blank response, the simple line I found so theatrically vexing: "Behold, he is in your power." And suddenly it hits me. God's words are sentimentally inscrutable because they speak to a condition beyond "the pin-ions and plumage" of sentimental love, beyond the most compre-hensive and sophisticated version of the theology of reward and punishment – in an important sense, beyond good and evil. The cold and unhesitating wager with Satan is the wager of existence itself. The Job praised with such evident pride is a quantum of God's fury pressed into place, "filtered and distilled as the purity of a man." But that determination, that gift of selfhood, of exis-tence, like the gifts God makes to the morning stars and the constellations, to the sea, to the offspring of the ostrich laid on the warm earth, is by its very nature exposed to the possibility of destruction.

I want to suggest to you that this is the truth of the event we grasped originally as despair pouring out of Job's proto-Stoicism. Round back of the heart sinking there – round back of the moment uncontainable sadness breaches the defence of reason

– is the wager of finite existence. Despair would be the simulacrum of that wager, its representation explicitly in terms of the refuges of personal history and universality it invades and appears to destroy. It drives Job toward the silence reported at 2:13, because it beggars the moral imagination that encompasses his understanding of the world. It drives him toward the silence reported at 40:4 – a silence he deliberately chooses, a renunciation of speech – because, in the storm-epiphany of God's words, he grasps the moral contradiction of his suffering as the logic of nature itself. Standing in the whirlwind, Job comes to the limit of the discourse that frames the entirety of the previous human dialogue, that accommodates his bitterness and his recalcitrance, that sanctions his call for a day in court. If the truth of despair – its genuine substance or content – is "reality point blank," if the logic of creation, the gift of life, requires his being left "to the earth," unprotected, what can he do but lay his hand on his mouth?

OBJECTION AND TRANSITION

"Wait a minute," I hear some disappointed reader object. "Surely there's at least one other option. Job could have resisted God right to the end. He could have refused the gift of life and sent it back. If the storm that ruins him blows through the logic of existence itself, he could have condemned and repudiated what is in its entirety." Perhaps. And yet, as you know, by the time God appears – by the time he addresses Job directly and demands a response – the hammer blow of such a condemnation has long since sounded. Repudiation of existence is not the climax of our protagonist's struggle, it's the beginning. "Let the day perish wherein I was born," he says at 3:3; "I loathe my life," at 7:16, 9:21, and 10:1. It is precisely the nihilism of this beginning that is forged by the fire of our author's poetry – first into the restless contradiction of bitterness, then into the paradox of faith, finally into the address of prayer that culminates in the epiphany of the whirlwind. By the time Job "lays his hand on his mouth" at 40:4, the repudiation of existence has been both posited and explicitly superseded. Job's discourse, the portrait of his integrity, of his endurance, of his patience, is nothing but the story of how his condemnation of existence is put aside, of how repudiation itself ultimately serves persistence; nothing (coming back to the language of Spinoza) but affirmation of the primacy of *conatus*. In the *Meditations on First Philosophy*, Descartes famously argues that the *ego cogito* is confirmed even in the act of doubting it.[11] That is why it can serve as the sure and certain foundation of all knowledge. The Book of Job makes the case for *conatus* in the same spirit. Our protagonist's complaints, his nihilism, are represented ultimately as modes of his endeavour to persist in his own being.

Come back now to the questions at hand: In what sense is it possible to imagine 40:6 to 41:34 as the truth of the event we grasped originally as persistence arising out of nihilism? In what would this truth – as truth – consist? The real object of investigation here is the counterpart of the suffering of limits I tried to describe when commenting on 38:1 to 40:2. The conclusion of that reflection was that the logic of finitude implies exposure to the fury of the external environment (the proverbial "heaving waters"). But there's a sense in which fury tests the limits of finite being from the inside as well, a sense in which God's power is present as the "actual essence" of "every leaf that trembles and every grain of sand."[12] Indeed, I want to suggest to you that the crowning phase of Job's epiphany is the apprehension of persistence, of *conatus*, as indwelling divinity, as what you might call immanent fury – and that the foundation of this fury is what you catch sight of in the knowing Spinoza conveys at the climax of his *Ethics* with the expression *amor Dei intellectualis*.[13] I want to suggest, in other words, that what Job comes to in the end, what he describes at 42:3 in terms of "things too wonderful for me, which I did not know," is the love of God. Walking the path to this conclusion requires, at a minimum, two things: an exposition of the immanent fury our author presents explicitly as the capstone of the whirlwind speeches, and an account of the logic of epiphany (supplementing the logic of finitude) that culminates in the recognition of love. Pursuing the first, you need to look at the strange encomiums to Behemoth (40:15–24) and Leviathan

(41:1–34); pursuing the second, at the arguments of Spinoza, sheltering in the term *conatus* itself.

IMMANENT FURY

A casual glance at our author's celebration of monsters seems only to reinforce Zapffe's description of Job's God. The prelude to it is a fresh blast on the theme of human impotence ("Deck yourself with majesty and dignity," the Lord bellows sarcastically, "then will I also acknowledge to you, that your own right hand can give you victory" – 40:10, 14). The already long list of production credits (for the morning stars, the constellations, the sky, the seas, day and night, life and death, the weather, etc.) is then extended to include the most powerful living creatures. The Almighty seems every inch "a braggart and blusterer." But I see at least two important differences in rhetorical strategy between 38:1 to 40:2 and 40:6 to 41:34.

First, whereas the theme of the opening speech was the imposition of limit and the concomitant exposure to the possibility of destruction, the theme of the conclusion is the power and majesty, the immanent force or fury, of the thing limited or created. Of Behemoth, God says:

Behold the strength of his loins, and his power in the muscles of his belly. He makes his tail stiff like a cedar; the sinews of his thighs are knit together. His bones are tubes of bronze, his limbs like bars of iron. (40:16–18)

Indeed, so great is his might that he can withstand the kinds of assaults that destroy human beings. Look at 40:21–23 – for all intents and purposes the inversion of Bugbee's story:

Under the lotus plants he lies, in the covert of the reeds and in the marsh. For his shade the lotus trees cover him; the willows of the brook surround him. Behold, if the river is turbulent he is not frightened; he is confident though Jordan rushes against his mouth.

Leviathan is praised at greater length. The impressive catalogue of his powers begins at 41:12:

> I will not keep silence concerning his limbs, or his mighty strength, or his goodly frame. Who can strip off his outer garment? Who can penetrate his double coat of mail? Who can open the doors to his face? Round about his teeth is terror. (41:12–14)

He too is impressively assault-resistant, especially in the face of human technology:

> Though the sword reaches him, it does not avail; nor the spear, the dart, or the javelin. He counts iron as straw, and bronze as rotten wood. The arrow cannot make him flee; for him slingstones are turned to stubble. Clubs are counted as stubble; he laughs at the rattle of javelins. His underparts are like sharp potsherds; he spreads himself like a threshing sledge on the mire. He makes the deep boil like a pot; he makes the sea like a pot of ointment. Behind him he leaves a shining wake; one would think the deep to be hoary. Upon earth there is not his like, a creature without fear. He beholds everything that is high; he is king over all the sons of pride. (41:26–30)

Melville's *Moby Dick* springs more or less whole from this passage, taking as its central theme what you might now conceive of as the tension between the divine and its simulacra embodied by Job's interlocutors. Captain Ahab is the apotheosis of the unfettered human imagination, the final station of the hubris you saw – first in the discourses of Eliphaz, Bildad, and Zophar, then in those of Elihu – heading toward a kind of rage against all resistance. And the whale that finally destroys him is precisely the creature our author describes, the vessel of an immanent divine fury lethally impervious to the transgressions of nineteenth-century human ingenuity.

But secondly, and on the other hand, whereas God claimed for himself the power of limitation or determination in the opening speech – reminding Job repeatedly of his own impotence, of the fact that there is only one creator of the world – the conclusion begins with the deliberate connection of our protagonist to the powers about to be celebrated, that is, with a Biblical version of the Platonic thesis that "all nature is akin": "Behold, Behemoth, which I made *as I made you*" (40:15, italics mine).

The suggestion, wild and terrifying as it is, is that what you're about to hear is a description of *conatus* fit for all creation. Among other things, this means that Behemoth and Leviathan are monsters, telling spectacles, in a double sense. They exhibit an immanent fury – but precisely as stand-ins for the "actual essence" of all finite beings. "Who has given to me that I should repay him," God says at 41:11 – effectively stepping outside the praise of Leviathan for a moment in order to clarify its purpose – "*Whatever is under the whole heaven is mine*" (italics mine). That is to say: the push back so obviously on display in Behemoth and Leviathan is also there in the "leaf that trembles," in the "grain of sand" – perhaps most importantly, in the patient sufferer. There: because indwelling divinity, immanent fury, belongs to being qua being. To follow the demonstration God gives between 40:15 and 41:34 is to see the divine substance of all nature pressed into the finite modes of its expression. It is to apprehend God in everything.

THE LOGIC OF EPIPHANY: SPINOZA'S *ETHICS*

How might we understand the structure of that apprehension? The question is crucial. If God's howling sermon on the nature of things is to be read as something other than the bluster of "a capricious cruel master who simply has no sense of universal justice," if we are to find in it, as per my wager, a love irreducible to the indifference we found at the bottom of the logic of finitude, we need to frame a logic of epiphany in which that love is essential. We need an account in which Job's own description of what God shows him – "things too wonderful for me, which I did not know" – may be taken in earnest and without apology as something other than the "sad metamorphosis" from "fighter" into "lamb." With this in mind, I want to look now at the arguments of Spinoza sheltering in the term *conatus*. They are unfolded in the treatise that has been on your radar since our first chapter: the *Ethics*.

The model for this treatise is Euclid's *Elements*, a far cry, needless to say, from the dramatic poetry of the Book of Job. Each section begins with a series of definitions and axioms, followed by a labyrinthine network of theorems or propositions on specified themes – metaphysics, epistemology, emotion, ethics, and politics, to name the most prominent. The idea I want to present as the capstone of the logic of epiphany – *amor dei intellectualis*, "the intellectual love of God" – arises only when everything else is on the table, in the final pages Spinoza dedicates to the discussion of human freedom.

A proper commentary on the arguments fronting those pages is neither possible nor desirable at this point. But if we suspend direct engagement of our author's text briefly, I can tell a campfire version of Spinoza's story, highlighting the connection between *conatus*/persistence/endurance and divine love in a way that deepens understanding of both Job's renunciation of speech (40:4) and his final benediction (42:2–6). Sit back, then, and indulge my philosophical enthusiasm. In the spirit of storytelling I'll try to keep technical details to a minimum.

Let's begin by sketching a context: If the history of philosophy from, say, the fourth century BCE to the dawn of the modern age in the scientific revolution of the seventeenth century, were a tale of adventure, the concept of "substance" would be its hero. The original Greek here is *ousia*, a word that goes back at least as far as Herodotus and means originally "what is your own," your "property" or "estate." In Aristotle's metaphysics and after, "substance" names a being's "stability" or "immutable reality," the "substratum" of all process and change. Both God and finite individual things are designated substances – the former strictly, the latter relatively or equivocally, for purposes of discriminating what is essential to a range of discrete phenomena (in biology, psychology, physics, etc.). Descartes, so revolutionary in other respects, maintains this equivocation, as if substance had two contending identities (universal and particular).

Spinoza's first and most important contribution to philosophy's tale is to insist that its hero always be "himself." If substance is primordial, he argues, it is one. Multiple substances may be distinguished only in reference to things that derive from them. They would follow, that is, from their accidents. But a substance that follows from its accidents would be subordinate – non-primordially primordial, an absurdity. Metaphysics proper begins, then, with the thought of a single substance, the infinite and eternal foundation of the real, the essence of nature, conceived of both as a creative fury (*Natura naturans*) and as the complete set of created things (*Natura naturata*).[14] It is just this substance that is properly and meaningfully called "God." The real point of departure for philosophy, in Spinoza's view, the unspoken truth of the Aristotelian tradition, is pantheism.

Not surprisingly, the disambiguation of substance has important consequences for how you understand the world and your place in it. What "is" will fall under one of three headings: a) God, b) divine attributes (that is, ways of conceiving of the essence of God – for example, as thought or as extension), or c) divine modes (that is, infinite or finite affections of God). All the bodies and ideas, all the things and persons I encounter in experience are manifestations of God conceived in accordance with one of the attributes. When I address you as another mind, I see you in light of the attribute of thought, when I meet you "in the flesh," in light of the attribute of extension. Granting this, Spinoza argues, you may resolve a persistent and troublesome dualism. Human beings are not ontologically independent immortal souls mysteriously reposing or sojourning in corruptible bodies. On the contrary, they are discrete modes of a single substance, conceivable under two attributes. What I call "mind" is nothing but an idea or awareness of the body; what I call body, nothing but the extended object of the mind. The succinct expression of this important resolution comes in Section 2, Proposition 13: "The object of the idea constituting the human mind is the body – i.e., a definite mode of extension actually existing, and nothing else."[15]

Analysis of the mind as the idea or awareness of the body yields, in turn, the possibility of three kinds of knowledge. To the extent that your awareness comprises impressions made on you by external objects of sense, (day)dream, or memory, you *imagine*. All sights, sounds, smells, tastes, and modes of physical contact, as well as the reveries and linguistic representations born of them, belong in this category. Imagination is the stuff of everyday life: "knowledge from casual experience."[16] It is also the single source of error. Your impressions often encourage or at least allow you to attribute the properties of your own body to other bodies (and vice versa). I think here of Heraclitus' saying, "the sun as to its size has the breadth of a human foot"[17] – a model of the epistemological failure Spinoza has in mind. Knowers go wrong when they confuse themselves with the outside world.

To the extent that you deliberately restrict yourself to understanding that world exclusively in terms of what Spinoza calls the "common properties"[18] of things, you *reason*. Reflection on common properties (as, for example, geometry reflects on the properties found in all extended bodies) circumvents the danger of (attribution) error. As a result, the claims of reason are always true. Mathematics and formal logic – that is, deduction from well-formed definitions and self-evident axioms – model this kind of knowledge. The *Ethics* itself also aspires to it, although, as a work wrought in the unruly medium of natural language, it cannot claim to avoid entirely the bias of either its author's or its readers' imaginations.

Finally, to the extent that you sometimes move in apprehension directly to the truth that reason delivers to you only by stepwise argument, you *intuit*. Intuition is an immediate grasp of the principle of the whole, of reality, as the immanent cause of individual things, the acknowledgment of God, of divine substance, as the ontological foundation of the everyday. The manner in which Spinoza formulates the possibility of this acknowledgment is instructive for our wider purposes. I cite the text of its introduction in the second *Scholium* of 2, 40:

Apart from these two kinds of knowledge (i.e. imagination and reason) there is, as I shall later show, a third kind of knowledge, which I shall refer to as "intuitive." This kind of knowledge proceeds from an adequate idea of the formal essence of certain attributes of God to an adequate knowledge of the essence of things.[19]

If I were actually telling Spinoza's story fireside, I'd want to pause here, poke at the embers in front of us, and watch the sparks fly upward. I'd want to let his words hang for a while in the air – then have them settle naturally over our reading of the whirlwind speeches. Why? Because in my view this typically turgid formula gives you the structure of the very event you need to understand. The word-storms of 38:1 to 40:2 and 40:6 to 41:34, and the definition of intuition at *Ethics* 2, proposition 40, seem almost perfectly isomorphic. The text at 38:1 to 40:2 renders poetically "the formal essence of certain attributes of God" – his transcendent fury, his determination of what is, his creative force; 40:6 to 41:34, "the essence of things" – the indwelling *conatus* of Behemoth and Leviathan. But if that is so, then, confirming the wager of this philosophical interlude, Spinoza elaborates precisely the logic of the epiphany in which the Book of Job culminates. Let's follow his account of intuition to the end. It is there, assuming the parallel holds up, that you'll find the bridge from divine fury to human wonder; and so there that you'll be in a position to decide for yourself whether Job's crossing constitutes a redemption or "a sad metamorphosis."

Sections 1 and 2 of the *Ethics* treat of metaphysics and epistemology respectively. Section 3 presents a developed philosophy of the emotions. This, as I said in passing near the end of the first chapter, is the stage upon which the idea of *conatus* makes its entrance. Your endeavour to persist in your own being is both the condition and the measure of your emotional experience. All emotions, as it turns out, are "affections of the body by which the body's activity is increased or diminished, assisted or checked, together with the ideas of these affections";[20] states, that is, in which the *conatus* waxes or wanes. In this sense, your "actual essence"[21] really is, in Spinoza's view, a kind of immanent fury, an indwelling fire kindled or quenched in response to the bodily states represented in your ideas.

Some forty determinate emotional states (wonder, contempt, devotion, derision, hope, fear, confidence, despair, joy, pity, compassion, and humility, for example) are analyzed in the propositions of Section 3 and catalogued in its appendix.[22] But there is also a general template immediately useful for the argument I am making: Any emotion/idea by which the body's activity is increased, by which the *conatus* is assisted, is pleasant; any emotion/idea by which the body's activity is decreased, by which the *conatus* is checked, is painful. What you regard as an object of pleasure, you love; what you regard as an object of pain, you hate.[23]

It is easy enough to see how the ideas of imagination might fill out this template. Your impressions are invariably pleasant or painful to some degree. And their objects are approved or rejected accordingly. Crucial to Spinoza's argument, though, is the claim that *all* modes of awareness have an emotional charge. Among other things, that means: the ideas of reason and intuition have an impact on *conatus* as well. Understanding the world is not affectively neutral. But neither, on reflection, may it be conceived as painful to any degree. As an activity in its own right, it always assists the *conatus* of the knower. Coming to the truth by reason or intuition, therefore, is ontologically empowering. It feeds the indwelling fire of your persistence or endurance, confirming and extending your immanent fury. In the final proposition of Section 3, Spinoza writes simply: "Among all the emotions that are related to the mind in so far as it is active, there are none that are not related to pleasure or desire."[24]

What are the implications of this argument for intuition in particular? Its attendant pleasure nurtures in you a love for what you regard as its object. But the object of intuition is always "the formal essence of certain attributes of God." Accordingly, intuition culminates in what Spinoza calls *amor Dei intellectualis* – the intellectual love of God.[25] The love of God is "the highest *conatus* of the mind."[26] No object imaginable is more conducive to understanding, to coming to the truth, and so to "the body's power of activity" reflected in all modes of knowledge. To see God in things is to apprehend the very substance of what they are. For the same reason, the love of God is "the highest possible contentment of mind."[27] No object imaginable could bring you greater or more lasting pleasure.

But: if Spinoza's formula for intuition expresses the structure of epiphany, if it is the philosophical correlate of the experience our author poetizes in the whirlwind speeches, then Job's sojourn as a sufferer cannot help but culminate in the love of God. The force of the whirlwind, as it turns out, is the perfection of his own patience, of his endurance, of the persistence that arises even out of his initial nihilism. And his final words of gratitude – "Therefore I have uttered things I did not understand, things too wonderful for me which I did not know" – are not "inexplicable in literary terms." On the contrary, they are the inevitable benediction of all genuine revelation. As his "fierce vision"[28] closes, Job "has seen the master's hand" – in Behemoth, in Leviathan, in the indwelling power of "whatever is under the whole heaven," in his own *conatus*. The voice from the whirlwind has carried him to "the highest possible contentment of mind," not by meeting or assuaging his complaints in the discourse of moral theology, but by showing him directly and immediately the divine nature of life itself. I think of a saying of Kafka's – number eighty-three of *The Zürau Aphorisms* – that compasses what is at stake in this exchange, projecting simultaneously the ground of our protagonist's repentance I suggested in discussion of the Bugbee story:

> We are sinful, not only because we have eaten of the Tree
> of Knowledge, but also because we have not yet eaten of the
> Tree of *Life*. The *condition* in which we find ourselves is
> sinful, guilt or no guilt.[29] (italics mine)

The apotheosis of suffering – at least in Job's case – addresses and corrects this failure.

Here, in my mind's eye, our disappointed reader comes to the end of his patience: "A tour of Spinoza's *Ethics*?" I imagine him saying. "On your account that's just the long way to a state of affairs sun-clear in the prologue! Does Job love God? Of course he does. His life is the model of religious devotion. That's why

God presents him to Satan, not once, but twice, as an exemplar of human service. Job's love endures even in the despair of nihilism. Indeed, his bitterness makes sense only as a response to betrayal of what he takes to be an intimate relationship. The problem with love in the Book of Job isn't on the human side. It lies with God himself. To put it bluntly: It's not that there's no evidence of Job loving God. The problem, the thing the Talmud records as having driven Rabbi Johanan to tears,[30] that scandalizes Wiesel and a host of modern readers, is that there's no evidence of God loving Job. It's this void, uncompensated, that provokes Zappfe's reference to God's "qualitative baseness" and makes Job's capitulation in the face of his brute force "sad," undignified. Let's have no more equivocation on the phrase "love of God." The single question Spinoza or anyone charting the territories of the Job story must answer is: Where, in the midst of the whirlwind, in the "heaving waters" of experience, in our blood-drenched clashes with the Sabeans, the Chaldeans, and their contemporary equivalents, do we see God's love for us?

The fire has burned low. As I speak in the voice of my imagined reader, I lean towards you into its retreating warmth. It strikes me, suddenly – having formulated the argument – that, for him, the summit of Job's insight is attained in bitterness, that is, nostalgia for moral universality in the face of a God whose actions are now inscrutable, irreconcilable with righteousness and personal integrity. He hears in Job's complaint, in his demand for a day in court, the final word on theology, on religious experience. The idea that a phenomenology of suffering would silence that voice seems both unlikely and undesirable. Unlikely: because my imagined reader is determined to have a *moral* explanation of what our author regards ultimately as an ontological problem. Undesirable: because, the lessons of ontology notwithstanding, moral discourse in the deepest sense – that is, respectful address of what is at stake in our human *ethos* – is indispensable to making ourselves at home in relationships, communities, and states. That our author himself intends this discourse to persist as relevant, even as he takes us beyond it, seems clear on the basis of the celebrated epistemological claim at 28:28: "Behold, the fear of the Lord, that is wisdom; *and to depart from evil is understanding*" (italics mine). I'll say more about the nature of this persistence in reflecting on God's final commendation of Job at 42:7. Just now, though – hands out over the coals – something important remains to be said on behalf of Spinoza. It concerns the climax of those arguments sheltering in the term *conatus* in which the character of God's love is specifically addressed.

Key here is a set of three propositions that complete the logic of Job's epiphany while clarifying the ground of my imagined reader's disappointment. The first is Section 5, 17: "God is without passive emotions, and he is not affected with any emotion of pleasure or pain."[31]

The premises that produce this conclusion are drawn from Spinoza's pantheistic metaphysics (*Ethics* 1), his analysis of imagination (2), and the template for emotion (3). God is an all-encompassing, infinite substance. As all-encompassing, he cannot be subject to the impressions of external bodies. There is nothing outside of him. As infinite, he is perfect. There is in him no negation or determination, no lack. As a result, the divine *conatus* is always unlimitedly affirmed – it waxes infinitely out of its own resources. But that means in turn that there is no person or thing God might regard as a source of pleasure. Hence the corollary to the same proposition: Strictly speaking, God cannot love or hate anyone.[32]

What you have here is the systematic explanation of divine indifference, supplementing, on the side of divine consciousness, the logic of finitude I sketched above reflecting on the poetry of Chapters 38 to 41. There is in God no sentimental love. The ground of any such love would be a passion irreconcilable with his perfection. Still – and this is crucial – God's sentimental indifference, his lack of passion, should not – cannot – be taken as evidence that there is in him no love at all. On the contrary, *amor Dei intellectualis* is the essence of what you might call God-consciousness, the constitutive state of a *conatus* unlimitedly affirmed in immediate self-knowledge. This is why, in Section 5, 35, Spinoza says: "God loves himself with an infinite intellectual love."[33] The divine mind discovers itself in every moment as the infinite source and sanction of its own persistence. God's experience, you could say, is enduring and unlimited epiphany.

Now, take the final step: this unlimited epiphany is not ontologically other than Job's epiphany, than the intuitions he, you, or I might have as finite beings. God is the substance of everything that is. Human epiphanies, accordingly, must be, one and all, modes of divine self-knowledge, like so many expressions on a single face. In the end, after long and careful preparation, Spinoza hurls this thunderbolt at his readers with a clarity, force, and directness you could scarcely have imagined possible, groping your way through the abstractions of his metaphysics:

> The mind's intellectual love towards God is the love of God wherewith God loves himself not in so far as he is infinite, but in so far as he can be explicated through the essence of the human mind considered under a form of eternity. That is, the mind's intellectual love towards God is part of the infinite love wherewith God loves himself.[34]

I think once more of Peter's adaptation of the prologue, this time of the ending that so took me by surprise. J.B. pirouettes from the piano stool to the floor; God on one side, Job on the other. Pantheism as dramatic spectacle! And finally, it clicks. The love of God, on Spinoza's account, is equivocal in its very nature. It flows out of human individuals, out of "the human mind," precisely as a manifestation – as a mode – of "the infinite love wherewith God loves himself," as the self-affirmation that constitutes life as such! In this regard, it cannot come to Job, or to you or me, as a gift of some determinate other, like the sheltering embrace of your human father. That is precisely what Spinoza rules out in Section 5, Proposition 17. Rather it surges up in Job, in you, or in me as life abundant, as the truth of the *conatus* that drives each and every affection of divine substance. Retracing the anatomy of patience (Chapters 3 to 31), I suggested to you that our author elaborates in the person of Job a non-linear relation of discourses, awareness of which invites you to apprehend in his every word the philosophical architecture of the space we first intuit distending out of his original cry of despair at 3:3. Behind that nihilism, as the dialogue reveals, is the shivering constancy of bitterness; behind that bitterness the still image of the Kierkegaardian absurd (faith); behind that absurdity – affirming its truth not by argument but by living presence – the talk with God (prayer). The lesson of the whirlwind is that this architecture, excavated entirely, bridges the gap between the human and the divine. Behind the talk with God, if my reading of 40:2 to 41:34 has any merit, is the intuition of his divinity in things; behind that intuition, accepting Spinoza's argument, his infinite self-love. I could put the conclusion here another way, exchanging the technical language of philosophy for a more familiar traditional vocabulary. The truth of patience is *agape* – a love that ultimately discovers the object of its longing safely and unassailably accommodated in the act of reaching towards it.

OUR HYPOTHESIS AGAIN ...

Take this as a sketch of Job's epiphany, speculative, certainly, but offered in what I hope you will recognize as an attempt at hermeneutical generosity: reading Chapters 38 to 41, we follow our protagonist backstage of his own suffering. The truth of his despair, of the sadness you see pouring out of his proto-Stoicism (1:21, 2:10), is revealed to him as the constitutional indifference implicit in the wager of existence itself. The truth of his patience, of the persistence you see arising out of his original nihilism (3:3), is the love of God, where this means both "the highest possible contentment of mind" and communion with "the infinite love wherewith God loves himself." Indifference and love, then: love and indifference – two forces at war in the generative, Heraclitean, sense in and as life itself; neither one subordinated to or subsumable by its putative opposite. And the struggle in its entirety – all of it – apprehended only from the standpoint of a genuine righteousness both confounded and surpassed. These are the "things too wonderful" that Job acknowledges at 42:3.

To this remarkable content we must add finally, and most importantly, recollection of the form of the experience our author presents. The arguments subtending the poetry of the Book of Job are sublime in the Kantian sense. They show us the violent contradiction of our protagonist's epiphany from a distance, in the reassuringly placid image of the word. But behind that spectacle, backstage of it – in an inchoate moment of wordless adrenaline – we must imagine a terrifying crosswind blowing at once, somehow, from the opposite directions of indifference and love into the single, still, and ineffable point of the sufferer's insight.

Job Is Restored

FROM SILENCE TO SILENCE

"That's how it is," said my old friend, taking Job's experience as the template of his own distress. "We find ourselves put to the test." My hypothesis as a reader has been that this disposition is, in a certain sense, our author's sole motif, the centre of the storm he wants to describe under the heading of human suffering. You apprehend it first in his prologue, as an existential contradiction at odds (as perhaps all genuine contradictions are) with the modes of its expression. Job's proto-Stoic voicing of persistence turns out to be the element of his despair. His cry of nihilistic despair turns out to be the element of his persistence. At the outset of the poem, our author takes pains to show you that the disposition of suffering turns its back on speech, that an adequate description of it will require him to play these discursive reversals against themselves, to wring from words those truths their day jobs as signifiers conceal, to follow them back – beyond explanation and lament, beyond all talking – to the point at which they show themselves finally, in a Conrad-inspired phrase of Henry Bugbee's, "massive with the vast silence from which they emerge."[1]

In fact, the considerable weight of the Book of Job comes to rest, as I have tried now to argue, on two moments of that "vast silence." The first, recorded at 2:13 ("and no one said a word to him for they saw that his suffering was very great"), frames for you the intersection of despair and persistence in Job's life, grasped as a project of moral agency. Here the interlocutors are simply carried to the limit of consolatory speech. The second, recorded at 40:4 ("I lay my hand on my mouth"), frames for you acknowledgment of the equally primordial forces of love and indifference. Here Job chooses silence explicitly in response to revelation of the ineffable foundation of pain. Silence to silence, then, and everything in between a work of dramatic irony, of movement in stasis, designed to retrace the turn in suffering – *of* suffering – from the first wordlessness to the second, from mute despair to the reticence of authentic human wisdom.

Everything in between – that is to say, Job's dialogue with Eliphaz, Bildad, and Zophar, the arguments of Elihu, even God's sermons of fury and love. In each of these complex discourses, the spoken word bodies forth as the retraction of or withdrawal from what it expresses. The friends' attempts at comfort – a detailed representation of the logic of Job's proto-Stoicism – culminate in rage. Job's renunciation of life – the bitter expression of his nihilism – culminates in his famous patience. Elihu's radicalized theology of reward and punishment – an emendation of the friends' piety – culminates in a Satan-style totalizing of the simulacra of the imagination. God's reasoning – the spirit of which I tried to catch above, in conversation with Bugbee and Spinoza – blows away in a literal whirlwind. From the end of the prologue to the climax of our protagonist's epiphany, the Book of Job gives you the spoken word in a kind of continual backward flight. Its art consists in making speech subject, even as spoken, to the gravity of a telling silence. Its central message is that being "put to the test" requires you to go behind the descent of that silence in existential contradiction to the self-conscious embrace of its truth.

Is it possible to extend the arc of this reading, finally, over the epilogue of the Book of Job? What remains of the text is a work in three short movements: our protagonist's final words (42:2–6), God's judgment of Eliphaz, Bildad, and Zophar, contrasting their failure with Job's success (42:7–9), and the restoration of Job's fortunes (42:10–17). In all, sixteen verses: and yet at each stage of our author's conclusion, there is at least the appearance of a challenge to the sense I've tried to make of previous chapters.

Job's final words seem to efface the renunciation of speech at 40:4, to undo almost immediately his hard-won choice of silence. Although you can account for God's dissatisfaction with Job's friends, his unqualified praise of our protagonist's talk seems at odds with the expression of his original provocation, paraphrased closely by Job himself in the end. ("Who is this that darkens counsel by words without knowledge?" God roars at 38:2. "Who is it that hides counsel without knowledge?" Job asks rhetorically at 42:3.) Finally, the restoration of fortunes seems to counter the principle of ontological indifference, reviving the suspicions of the disappointed reader, namely, that God toys with human beings for his own amusement, that he is a conscienceless bully, capable of anything, including the alleviation of suffering, if the spirit moves. How do you make sense of these things?

JOB'S FINAL WORDS

We've looked already, tracking through the whirlwind speeches, at parts of Job's final intervention. I suggested, for example, that the "things too wonderful" celebrated at 42:3 refer us to the apprehension of the Almighty's immanent fury – first and most evidently in the monstrous power of Behemoth and Leviathan, then, by extension, in all creation; that they mark the apotheosis of epiphany as the perception of God in "every leaf that trembles," "every grain of sand," in short, every *conatus* that persists in its own being. I suggested, unpacking Bugbee's story of the man in the river, that Job's vow to "repent in dust and ashes" at 42:6 expresses his acknowledgment of a truth in being, of a "reality point blank," that outstrips moral imagination: recognition that the mistake of his own bitterness was the stubborn determination to capture the meaning of God's fury in a discourse, the limitations of which he himself had tagged in criticism of his friends' theology. Both phrases convey a profound revolution of understanding, a kind of testimony to the transformative character of genuine religious experience.

But a closer look at the sequence of 42:2–6, as a whole, reveals a more intimate relation to Job's epiphany as concretely lived. Here is the text in full, divided for purposes of clarifying its structure:

1 I know that thou canst do all things and that no purpose of thine can be thwarted.
2 "Who is it that hides counsel without knowledge?"
3 Therefore, I have uttered what I did not understand, things too wonderful for me which I did not know. ·
4 "Hear and I will speak; I will question you, and you declare to me."
5 I had heard of thee by the hearing of the ear, but now my eyes see thee; therefore, I despise myself and repent in dust and ashes.

What you have in this passage seems to me a deliberate and perfect epitome of Job's sojourn as a sufferer. The countenance of "things too wonderful," of the direct perception of God in creation, is situated, appropriately, at the centre (sentence 3 above). It is bounded on either side by explicit *mimeses* of the voice of God (sentences 2 and 4) recalling 38:2 and 38:3 to 40:7 respectively. It is as if Job were saying, "here is the reflection of my ineffable vision in words, the mirror of my epiphany" or "my speech now is a simulacrum of the experience that drove me to silence." This is already quite marvellous. But at the widest orbit (sentences 1 and 5) our protagonist marks in addition the stations of bitterness and *amor Dei* that the voice from the whirlwind binds miraculously together. The statement "I know that thou canst do all things and that no purpose of thine can be thwarted" recalls the advocacy of God's sublimity at odds with the nostalgia for moral universality characteristic of Job's position throughout the dialogue with Eliphaz, Bildad, and Zophar. The statement "I had heard of thee by the hearing of the ear, but now my eyes see thee" expresses with superb efficiency the difference between the mediated reflections of the transcendental imagination at work in all versions of moral theology (including Job's) and the immediate apprehension of "reality point blank" that comes in those terrifying moments where the pretense of imagination is shattered. That is to say: Job's final intervention gathers up in five sentences the whole of his movement from nihilism (3:3) to repentance (42:6).

But now, rejoining the challenge I remarked above: why return, in conclusion, to discursive representation of an experience our protagonist chose deliberately to address non-discursively? Why produce a simulacrum – however elegant – of Job's silent apprehension of God's indifference/love? Or again: If wordlessness truly stands at the centre of our author's phenomenology of suffering, what does he have to gain by word-mirroring 40:4 at 42:2–6? Something, it seems to me, like the opportunity of penning a final chapter in the story of patience. You've followed that narrative at this point from its inception as unacknowledged persistence, through the loss of refuge, up through bitterness, faith, and prayer, to divine love. But, on reflection, there is one more aspect of this definitively human integrity that requires your attention. It presents itself the moment *amor Dei* goes to work, the moment the sufferer – having endured to the end as Job does – comes again to the doors of human refuge; the moment the original trajectory of suffering is reversed, bringing the *conatus* – tempered by its pain – back to the histories and universalities in terms of which it must root itself in the world once more moving forward; the moment, gathering all of this into a single word, you begin to *heal*.

I want to suggest to you that healing is the culmination of patience, not in the sense that it goes beyond *amor Dei* – love is ontologically ultimate – but in the sense that it constitutes that love's comprehensible presence in our lived and shared experience. The leading edge of this presence is the restoration of speech. Healing requires the accommodation of epiphany in those narratives, personal and universal, in terms of which we make ourselves at home in the world. Job speaks in the epilogue – for himself, to God, and on behalf of his friends – as an attestation of his homecoming. But far from letting words substitute for the reality he has seen, at this point with his own eyes, he makes them transparent to their source. He invites you to *look back through them*, precisely to "the vast silence from which they emerge." There's another way of describing this transformation

– harbouring in sentence 3 itself – that recuperates the claim I made at the outset of this study regarding the Book of Job's pedigree as a philosophical work. Job's final intervention is spoken in wonder – an attitude we can now credit, in the spirit of our author, as apprehending and affirming in things at once their fragility and their divinity.

GOD'S JUDGMENT

It is just this attitude, ultimately, that separates Job from his friends. Here is a point of departure for making sense of God's judgment of Eliphaz, Bildad, and Zophar at 42:7–8 – one of the most oracular passages in the entire poem. I cite all of 42:7–9 in order to present it to you properly in the context of our author's narrative:

> After the Lord had spoken these words to Job, the Lord said to Eliphaz the Temanite: "My wrath is kindled against you and against your two friends; for you have not spoken of me what is right, as my servant Job has. Now therefore take seven bulls and seven rams, and go to my servant Job, and offer up for yourselves a burnt offering; and my servant Job shall pray for you, for I will accept his prayer not to deal with you according to your folly; for you have not spoken of me what is right, as my servant Job has. So Eliphaz the Temanite and Bildad the Shuhite and Zophar the Na'amathite went and did what the Lord had told them; and the Lord accepted Job's prayer.

The riddling key line is repeated for emphasis:

> [F]or you have not spoken of me what is right, as my servant Job has. (42:7, 42:8)

As I said before, it is possible, on the basis of my reading of previous chapters, to give an account of how the friends miss the mark. Their theology is dictated entirely by limited and limiting exercise of the moral imagination, that is, by the Satanic reduction of human experience to reward and punishment. On such a view, God is first and foremost a transcendent judge, not an immanent cause or creator. And Job's suffering is the consequence of an unspecified sin. But – the voice from the whirlwind shatters this theological position. And the prologue rules out its specific application. That is, long before the judgment of 42:7–9, the narrative itself enjoins you to conclude that Eliphaz, Bildad, and Zophar are wrong about God in general and about his relation to Job in particular.

More difficult for me, especially working through the text in the early stages of this study, was making sense of God's unqualified praise of our protagonist: "for you have not spoken of me what is right *as my servant Job has*." To what exactly does the Almighty here refer? By the time he stakes this claim, Job has said many things *of* and *to* him. If you assume he has in mind particular statements ("I know that thou canst do all things and that no purpose of thine can be thwarted," for example), the opening volley of the whirlwind speech ("Who is this that darkens counsel by *words without knowledge?*") appears to take everything Job says prior to Chapter 38 out of play. But that leaves only 40:2–6 and its mirror at 42:2–6 as possible objects of divine approbation, and forces you to read even these passages not as culminating expressions of a finely wrought character but as clean breaks with an attitude now (that is, in the face of epiphany) thoroughly discredited. Indeed, it puts you in a position very much like the one Wiesel deplores – having saved the "lamb" at the expense of the "fighter"; having interpreted God's blessing as endorsement of a character famous for integrity, who, under pressure, flailing in the river of his own suffering, finally and sadly knuckles under.

Mulling over this problem now late in the game, it occurs to me that the unity of our author's compositional vision is better served in taking the content designated by "what is right" to be the discursive anatomy of endurance I tried to trace in Chapter Three, that existential line of intensity that runs up through bitterness to faith, then to prayer, then to love blossoming finally in the healing wonder of 42:3. In this view, what God approves in Job's speech is not one or more propositions but a *logos*, the indispensable origin of which is that discord, already distending out of the cry of despair at 3:3, between the protagonist's recognition of divine sublimity and his righteousness "in his own eyes." Accepting such a hypothesis, in turn, would permit you to draw three additional conclusions: 1) that the grand vision of Job's epiphany is essentially an unpacking of the transcendence of reason and imagination he already attributes to God in Chapter 9[2] – that is, that the story of Job's sojourn as a sufferer is really that of grasping concretely the meaning of the sublime; 2) that Job's personal righteousness, though not sufficient protection against the consequences of the wager of existence, is nevertheless necessary for taking its true measure, the still point in terms of which he compasses the storm of his misfortune and which persists through all forms of existential contradiction; and 3) that the healing of wonder, the culmination of Job's *logos*, of his patience or endurance, of his *conatus*, is not – as Plato and Aristotle were later to argue – the beginning of philosophy, but its end. On the authority of the Book of Job, the deepest and truest understanding of life takes things at once in their fragility and divinity, letting this vision dictate both word and deed.

GENEROSITY – HUMAN AND DIVINE

Chapter 42 provides almost nothing in the way of a portrait of what you might call the interiority of such an understanding. Describing Job's restoration, our author reverts to the objective, stone-like impenetrability of the language of the prologue, as if to signal explicitly his rejoining of the established tale polished by the retelling of many generations:

> And the Lord restored the fortunes of Job, when he had
> prayed for his friends; and the Lord gave Job twice as much
> as he had before. Then came to him all his brothers and sisters
> and all who had known him before, and ate bread with him
> in his house; and they showed him sympathy and comforted

him for all the evil that the Lord had brought upon him; and
each of them gave him a piece of money and a ring of gold.
And the lord blessed the latter days of Job more than his
beginning; and he had fourteen thousand sheep, six thousand
camels, a thousand yoke of oxen, and a thousand she-asses.
He had also seven sons and three daughters. And he called
the name of the first Jemimah; and the name of the second
Keziah; and the name of the third Kerenhappuch. And in all
the land there were no women so fair as Job's daughters; and
their father gave them inheritance among their brothers.
And after this Job lived a hundred and forty years, and saw
his sons, and his sons' sons, four generations. And Job died,
an old man, and full of days. (42:10–17).

Here as at the outset, we see things from the outside. Job's social
world returns. His possessions are multiplied. He is once again
the father of children, the patriarch of an extended family. And
yet – there is one hint of what healing wonder might have fos-
tered in him inwardly. It comes in the second clause of the first
sentence of the passage just cited: "And the Lord restored the
fortunes of Job, *when he had prayed for his friends*" (italics mine).

The statement refers you back to verses 8 and 9, of course,
where Job's intervention is stipulated as a condition for the possibility of God's appeasement in the face of the comforters' failure to speak "what is right" of him. It seems to me important for
grasping the philosophical thrust of the epilogue for at least three
reasons. First, it reinforces the proper end of the existential line
of intensity running through the stages of our protagonist's
patience. The persistence that begins in bitterness ends in prayer.
It is important, having found Job "put to the test," struggling in
despair, to leave him in the act our author takes to be the truth of
his integrity. Second, it captures that integrity "on the job" as an
act of intercession – implying, at least by juxtaposition, that healing wonder makes itself manifest in the care for and comfort of
others, that the fruit of prayer is generosity. And third, just in this
respect, it retraces the orbit of human kindness discernible first in
the mute solidarity of those seven days and nights Eliphaz, Bildad,

and Zophar dedicate to the suffering Job, as if to suggest that generosity – as opposed to judgment or ideology, as opposed to rage – were the *alpha* and *omega* of human relations.

The idea of an all-embracing generosity, finally, could provide the key to grasping fully our author's report of the restoration of reputation, property, and family that follows Job's intercession (42:11–13). In a work animated at all levels by the mirror-play of divine reality and its human simulacra, it would be surprising indeed to find no prototype for Job's gesture of accommodation – for the expression of his healing wonder – in God's grandeur. If human generosity is the *alpha* and *omega* of moral and political life – of our relations with others – we might expect, in conclusion, some suggestion that divine generosity constitutes the widest orbit of creation – of being – itself. Here is one way of reading our author's strategy, reprising the style and content of the ancient tale: on the heels of God's self-revelation in Chapters 38 to 41, it must echo in its own way the transcendence of moral imagination effected in the body of the work. That is to say, just as behind Job's despair you found the wager of finite existence, just as behind Job's persistence you found the imminent fury of divine love, behind his restoration you must find the original *gift* of creation.

That transcendent or primordial giving – a thing prior to the entire economy of reward and punishment, prior to any obligation God might be imagined to have to Job qua servant – cannot be conceived of as an arbitrary breach of the principle of indifference. On the contrary, both indifference and love open out of it. Or again, prior versions of the story perhaps notwithstanding,[3] Job's restoration ought not be read merely as the morally warranted restitution of an individual, still less the spoonful of sugar in a story otherwise unbearably dark. Rather, you should apprehend our protagonist's happy ending as laid, Euripides-style, over the original gift, thanks to which both his despair and his persistence are possible. Near the end of a long career dedicated to restoring the question of being as meaningful for and central to contemporary philosophy, Heidegger found the key to expressing the ungrounded primacy of his subject – the *alpha* of fundamental ontology, already concealed and forgotten in the traditional interpretations of being as idea, substance, subject, spirit, will to power, etc. – in a common locution of his own language. For speakers of German, the simplest, most straightforward affirmation of being would be: *Es gibt das Sein*.[4] We translate this: "There is being." But the *es gibt* means literally "it gives." The absolute priority of generosity – as regards being per se, and so as regards being in all of the modalities that the Book of Job shows us – is thus reflected in the common parlance of his native tongue, a fact in which Heidegger took some pride. But whether it is reflected in common parlance or not, our author seems determined to leave us with the thought that God is generous.

PHILOSOPHICAL GRANDFATHERS: CONCLUSION

"A poet makes himself responsible for the *living reality* of his narratives. And everything in poetry ought to bear witness to *that* responsibility." In the silence that follows these words, the midday heat seems literally to ring – in spite of the awning stretching out over us and other tables nearby.

"I'm staggered by *your* bearing witness," I want to say. I see the original tale suddenly, in my mind's eye, as an old house he has renovated so imaginatively, so expertly, that spaces in it you would have taken for granted as commonplace now seem capable of holding extraordinary things. He has made room, somehow, for despair to pour out and persistence to arise, for earnest comfort to decline into rage, for bitterness to ascend into prayer, for the sky of the human imagination to clear and the storms of God to ignite, for incalculable loss and its healing, for cosmic indifference and cosmic love and cosmic generosity – above all, perhaps, for telling silence. "All there," I think. "All there in a story that, having arrived on his doorstep in whatever way that happened, might have taken fifteen minutes to pass along."

As with the tale, so also its characters, vivid and fully formed in their own right, while at the same time full of the open space of literary possibility. In the Biblical Job is the seed of tragic and comic heroes to come – Shakespeare's Lear, for example, Voltaire's Candide. Satan is surely the prototype of Goethe's

Mephistopheles. How much of the feckless friendship dramatized in Stoppard's *Rosenkrantz and Guildenstern Are Dead* is already framed in the failure of Eliphaz, Bildad, and Zophar? How much of the poetic imagination Kundera indicts in *Life Is Elsewhere* as the unwitting stooge of totalitarian rage is already visible in the character of Elihu? The narrator of *Moby Dick*, as I mentioned in passing above, identifies himself explicitly with the messengers of the prologue, as if, after the Book of Job, narration itself were bound ineluctably to the report of catastrophe. Even our protagonist's dead children – destroyed, as it were, "offstage" – become prods in the literature of remembrance made necessary by the savage genocides of the twentieth century, the original nameless innocents who mustn't be forgotten.[5]

Finally, as with the characters, so also their questions – above all, in my own sojourn at least, the one about God's love. The Book of Job articulates something like the domain of that experience, but only the likes of you and me – trying to make sense of the accreted layers of our reading and formal education and the accidents, exigencies, and epiphanies of our own accommodations – can settle it. Here I think: "The Spinoza-tinged idea of *amor Dei* as the upsurge of life, as immanent fury, is beautiful and true. But there will always be a child in me somewhere who wants and needs ... help ... Another contradiction simply to be lived ..."

As these things tumble through my mind, I say, "Your story plants in me the very thing it comes to in the end: wonder at the idea of a person, of a life, of a world at once divine and fragile."

He smiles slightly: "That's what all stories come to, properly told." The words are even, offered, it seems to me, not so much in the spirit of instruction as of testimony. His voice is somehow both austere and kind.

Notes

PREFACE

1 Augustine, *St. Augustine's Confessions*, trans. William Watts (Cambridge: Harvard University Press, 1960), 463–5.
2 Cf. for example, Schmuel Vargon, "The Date of Composition of the Book of Job in the Context of S.D. Luzzato's Attitude to Biblical Criticism," *The Jewish Quarterly Review* 91, no. 3/4 (Jan.–Apr. 2001): 377–94.
3 In reflections to follow, I refer to the writer(s) of the Book of Job mostly as "our author." Where style makes a pronoun preferable, I use "he" in order to harmonize references with imagined conversations in Chapters 4 and 8 where I project on this writer (for both dramatic and philosophical purposes) the bearing of a retired male professor. Needless to say, as long as the identity of the writer(s) remains unknown, her/his/their gender(s) will remain unknown as well.
4 The RSV draws your attention to twenty-three such places.
5 Robert Gordis, *The Book of Job: Commentary, New Translation, and Special Studies* (New York: The Jewish Theological Seminary of America, 1978).

CHAPTER ONE

1 Cf. Martin Heidegger, *Being and Time*, trans. John Macquarrie and Edward Robinson (San Francisco: Harper and Row, 1962), esp. 78–122.
2 Cf. Martin Heidegger, *The Question Concerning Technology*, trans. William Lovitt (New York: Garland Publishing, 1977), 3–35.

3 Cf. Plato, *Republic*, trans. Paul Shorey, in *The Collected Dialogues of Plato*, eds. Edith Hamilton and Huntington Cairns (Princeton: Princeton University Press, 1961), esp. 357a–417b, 605–61.

4 Cf. for example, Plato, *Euthyphro*, trans. Lane Cooper, in *The Collected Dialogues of Plato*, 170–85.

5 Cf. Plato, *Crito*, trans. Hugh Tredennick, in *The Collected Dialogues of Plato*, 35–9. Here Socrates memorably channels the laws of Athens themselves. In the closing pages of the dialogue, they possess him, speaking through him in a kind of choral voice that condemns the escape proposed by Crito as an unconscionable betrayal of lifelong accommodation by the state.

6 I am indebted to David Seale – the colleague in question – for these lectures (delivered originally in 1998 at Bishop's University) and for many conversations on topics in Greek tragedy and philosophy over the past twenty years.

7 Franz Kafka, *The Trial*, trans. Willa and Edwin Muir (New York: The Modern Library, 1964), 262.

8 The Book of Job, 28:12. All citations of the Holy Bible are taken from the Revised Standard Version (New York: Thomas Nelson & Sons, 1952). The Book of Job, of course, is cited many times. For the reader's convenience, I include chapter and verse in the text itself.

9 Dante Alighieri, *Inferno*, trans. Allen Mandelbaum (New York: Bantam Books, 1982), 46–7.

10 The method of phenomenology privileges description over explanation. The goal is to follow as closely and sensitively as possible the way in which things actually come to light and present themselves in experience. In the introduction to *Being and Time*, Heidegger writes: "Phenomenology means ... to let that which shows itself be seen from itself in the very way in which it shows itself from itself." Cf. *Being and Time*, 58.

11 Baruch Spinoza, *Ethics*, trans. Samuel Shirley (Indianapolis: Hackett Publishing Company), 108.

12 In his commentary on the *Ethics*, Harry Wolfson tags forerunners of this idea in Hellenistic and medieval philosophy. Aquinas, for example, argues that "every natural thing aims at self-conservation," Duns Scotus that "every natural being desires with a natural desire to continue in existence." Dante remarks that "everything which exists desires its own existence." Cf. Harry Austryn Wolfson, *The Philosophy of Spinoza: Unfolding the Latent Processes of His Reasoning*, vol. 2 (New York: Schocken Books, 1969), cf. esp. 195–208.

CHAPTER TWO

1 Gordis, *The Book of Job*, 21.
2 Ralph Waldo Emerson, *Self-Reliance*, in *Essays and English Traits* (New York: P.F. Collier & Son, 1909), 70.
3 Gordis, *The Book of Job*, 580. Reviewing contending accounts of the composition of Book of Job, the author here cites N.H. Snaith.
4 Ibid., cf. 501–18.
5 Leviticus 10:1–7.
6 Leviticus 10:3.
7 The Book of Amos 8:11.
8 Plato, *Apology*, trans. Hugh Tredennick, in *The Collected Dialogues of Plato*, 40b, 24.
9 Cf. Plato, *Symposium*, trans. Michael Joyce, in *The Collected Dialogues of Plato*, 211c–23d, 563–74.
10 Cf. for example, Soren Kierkegaard, *Fear and Trembling*, trans. Alistair Hannay (London: Penguin Books, 1985), esp. 98–148.

CHAPTER THREE

1 William Shakespeare, *Twelfth Night*, in *Shakespeare's Comedies*, ed. David Bevington (New York: Pearson, 2007), 352.
2 Sophocles, *King Oedipus*, trans. E.F. Watling, in *The Theban Plays* (New York: Penguin Classics, 1947), 29.
3 Shakespeare, *Twelfth Night*, 369.
4 Sophocles, *King Oedipus*, 68.
5 Bob Dylan, "What Can I Do for You," lyric published in *The Definitive Bob Dylan Songbook* (New York: Amsco Publications, 2001), 736.
6 Dylan Thomas's poem "To Others than You" contains the evocative line: "My friends were enemies on stilts with their heads in a cunning cloud." Cf. *The Collected Poems of Dylan Thomas, 1934–1952* (New York: New Directions Publishing, 1957), 118. It catches beautifully the spirit of Job's criticism of his friends' attempts at comfort. Eliphaz's reason – his articulation of what is universal in the human condition – leaves no room for recognition of the persistence of Job's integrity.
7 Cf. G.W.F. Hegel, *The Philosophy of History*, trans. J. Sibree (Buffalo: Prometheus Books, 1991), 21.

CHAPTER FOUR

1 Henry Bugbee, *The Inward Morning* (Athens, GA: University of Georgia Press, 1999).

2 I am indebted here to Michele Murray, currently dean of Arts and Science at Bishop's University, who presented these pictures as part of a very memorable travelogue to a group of us, following an immersion course in French in the summer of 2011.

3 Cf. Max Horkheimer and Theodor W. Adorno, *The Dialectic of Enlightenment*, trans. John Cumming (New York: Seabury Press, 1969), 3.

4 Sophocles, *Antigone*, in *The Theban Plays*, 135–6. Its kindred spirit is evident in the opening stanzas:

> Wonders are many on earth, and the greatest of these
> Is man, who rides the ocean and takes his way
> Through the deeps, through the wind-swept valleys of perilous seas
> That surge and sway.
> He is master of ageless Earth, to his own will bending
> The immortal mother of gods by the sweat of his brow,
> As year succeeds to year, with toil unending
> Of mule and plough.
> He is lord of all things living; birds of the air,
> Beasts of the field, all creatures of sea and land
> He taketh, cunning to capture and ensnare
> With sleight of hand.

5 Soren Kierkegaard, *Fear and Trembling*, in *Selections from the Writings of Kierkegaard*, trans. Lee M. Hollander (Garden City, NY: Anchor Books, 1960), cf. 67–79.

6 Ibid., 145.

7 Cf. for example, Sam Harris, *The End of Faith* (New York: W.W. Norton & Company, 2004), or Christopher Hitchens, *God Is Not Great* (New York: Twelve, 2007).

8 Cf. Immanuel Kant, *Religion within the Bounds of Reason Alone*, trans. Theodore M. Greene & Hoyt H. Hudson (New York: Harper Torch Books, 1934).

CHAPTER FIVE

1 Elie Wiesel, *Messengers of God: Biblical Portraits and Legends*, trans. Marion Wiesel (New York: Simon and Schuster Paperbacks, 1976), xii.

2 Cf. Herman Melville, *Moby Dick* (New York: Grosset & Dunlop, 1925), 511.

3 The Flying Karamazov Brothers are a juggling/comedy/theatre troupe. Originally street artists, they have now performed on Broadway and around the world. Their version of Shakespeare's *Comedy of Errors* is accessible on YouTube.

CHAPTER SIX

1 Cf. Gordis, *The Book of Job*, 546–53.

2 Cf. Susan Schreiner, *Where Shall Wisdom Be Found?* (Chicago: The University of Chicago Press), 131.

3 Ibid., 132.

4 Wiesel, *Messengers of God*, 228.

5 Boethius, *Philosophiae Consolationis*, in Loeb Classical Library 74 (Cambridge: Harvard University Press, 1973), 224.

6 Cf. Maurice Merleau-Ponty, *The Phenomenology of Perception*, trans. Colin Smith (London: Routledge, 1962), 163–4.

7 Fyodor Dostoevsky, *The Brothers Karamazov*, trans. David McDuff (London: Penguin Books, 2003), 821.

8 The retelling of Job's story accomplished in the complete set of Blake's engravings is a powerful version of this resolution. There, Blake situates suffering itself in the realm of imagination. Job's odyssey is spiritual. In an explicitly and unapologetically Christian reading, we follow what the poet takes to be the upward path of our protagonist's faith from reliance on the book and the law to devotion to the living word.

CHAPTER SEVEN

1 Peter Wessel Zapffe, *Om Det Tragiske*, trans. Slavoj Žižek (Oslo: Aventura Forlag, 1983), 487–8. I am grateful to Filip Niklas for bringing the Žižek/Zapffe remarks to my attention.

2 Slavoj Žižek, *Event: Philosophy in Transit* (London: Penguin, 2014).

3 Wiesel, *Messengers of Gods*, 231.

4 Ibid., 233.

5 I am indebted here, again, to David Seale's lectures on Euripides' *Hecuba*, in which the analysis of the sequence of events was essential to grasping the playwright's meaning.

6 Cf. Ludwig Wittgenstein, *Tractatus Logico-Philosophicus*, trans. D.F. Pears and B.F. McGuinness (New York: Routledge & Kegan Paul, 1963), 151. There Wittgenstein writes:

> My propositions serve as elucidations in the following way: anyone who understands me recognizes them as nonsensical, when he has used them – as steps – to climb up beyond them. (He must, so to speak, throw away the ladder after he has climbed up it.) He must transcend these propositions, and then he will see the world aright.

7 Cf. T.S. Eliot, *Four Quartets* (London: Faber & Faber, 1944), 17. There Eliot writes:

> Words strain, crack and sometimes break, under the burden, under the tension, slip, slide, perish, decay with imprecision, will not stay in place, will not stay still.

8 Bugbee, *The Inward Morning*, 171–3.

9 Immanuel Kant, *Critique of Judgment*, trans. Werner Pluhar (Indianapolis: Hackett Publishing, 1987), 119–23.

10 Spinoza, *Ethics*, 155.

11 René Descartes, *Discourse on Method and Meditations*, trans. Laurence J. Lafleur (Saddle River: Prentice Hall, 1952), cf. especially 81–91.

12 Cf. *The Definitive Bob Dylan Songbook*, 187.

13 Cf. Spinoza, *Ethics*, 210–23. I discuss specific propositions related to this concept below.

14 Cf. ibid., 51–2.

15 Ibid., 71.

16 Ibid., 90.

17 Cf. Jonathan Barnes, *Early Greek Philosophy* (London: Penguin Books, 1988), 123.

18 Cf. Spinoza, *Ethics*, esp. 73, 87–90.

19 Ibid., 90.

20 Ibid., 103.

21 Ibid., 108.

22 Ibid., 113–51.

23 Ibid., 113.

24 Ibid., 139–40.

25 Ibid., 217.

26 Ibid., 214.

27 Ibid., 215.

28 I take this phrase from Rilke who intends in it a summary of human life. Cf. Rainer Maria Rilke, *Duino Elegies*, trans. David Young (New York: W.W. Norton & Company, 1992), 85.

29 Franz Kafka, *The Zürau Aphorisms of Franz Kafka*, trans. Michael Hoffman (New York: Schocken Books, 2006), 82.
30 Gordis, *The Book of Job*, 20.
31 Spinoza, *Ethics*, 210.
32 Ibid.
33 Ibid., 218.
34 Ibid., 218–19.

CHAPTER EIGHT

1 Bugbee, *The Inward Morning*, 54.
2 Cf. especially 9:10 – "[God] does great things beyond understanding, and marvelous things without number."
3 For a scholarly discussion of the relation of our author's text to folk-tale and other sources see Gordis, *The Book of Job*, 576–81.
4 Cf. Martin Heidegger, *On Time and Being*, trans. Joan Stambaugh (New York: Harper Torchbooks, 1972), 5.
5 Elie Wiesel makes this connection more or less explicitly in his criticism of the Book of Job's "third act." Cf. Wiesel, *Messengers of God*, 233–4.

Index